Dedicated to my family and to everyone who ever supported me and my work.

Table of Contents

Intro 1 -

I'm everywhere and nowhere. And I own nothing and everything.

I lived out of a backpack for the past 7 years. This is my story...

I never really had a place of my own. I never bought any furniture. The clothes I've been wearing for the past few months cost less than $20. The entire outfit. Including shoes.

I never owned a car. I don't have a smartphone. My most valuable possession is this laptop right here on which I write these words. It's a $300 Acer. That's really all I got.

Am I a minimalist? I don't know. I'm mostly just myself. To me, minimalism is just another way of selling us more expensive crap. Really, really expensive crap. Who needs a t-shirt for $60? I don't...

I think that a real minimalist doesn't talk about it. He just lives it. Oh, well, I guess I just broke that rule. Whatever.

Over the past few years I've lived in so many different places and cities that I can barely remember. And with living I mean a period of at least three months.

I just turned 32 a few weeks ago. I spend less than $800 a month including everything. Including food.

And health insurance. Sometimes I pay even less. Right now in Malaysia I spend around $600 a month.

I have enough. More than enough.

I have access to everything. I have access to more food than I'll ever be able to eat. I have access to more clothes than I will ever be able to wear. I have access to more water than I will ever be able to drink. While others don't have access to any of this.

Here's a question I've asked myself many times in the past few months...

Just because we have access to all of these things does that mean we really need to own or buy all of these things? I don't know.

For the past few days I've been living in one of these container hotels. You know, where all you got is a bed in some sort of container tube. At the same time I've been working in a coworking space with 24/7 access.

The bed costs $8 a night and the coworking space is around $50 a month. I have less than 10 things with me.

I have enough.

And sometimes I'm more happy. Sometimes I'm less happy. But I'm mostly just grateful to be alive.

Am I privileged? Of course, I am. And as you're reading this, chances are that you're privileged, too.

I live the lifestyle that I'm living partly out of necessity and partly because it's liberating.

Because it feels like freedom. At least sometimes. I can live, work, eat and sleep wherever I want to. All I have with me is a carry on bag with my stuff. And my laptop. And a Kindle. That's all I really need.

Ok, maybe I couldn't live in Manhattan anymore. Also, I wouldn't want to. Who wants to live in a cubicle for more than $2000 a month? Heck, that's my budget for 3 months. Including food. Including everything.

When I started this lifestyle a couple of years ago, I started it because I didn't have a lot of money. All I had to my name were around $20,000 that I saved over the years working various jobs. I basically saved everything I ever got my hands on. For my entire life. Until I was 26.

That's all I got when I started. I started this kind of lifestyle more than 7 years ago. Mostly because I was scared. I was scared of everything. I'm still scared. Sometimes.

I was scared that I would stay at the same job for too long and then they would fire me. And then no one would hire me because I was too "inbred". And then me and my future family would have to starve. I was seeing myself living on the streets.

The thought of having to rely on someone that could simply fire me when he or she pleases to, scared the shit out of me. It also scared the shit out of me to depend on a single person. Or in this case one company.

So about three years ago I quit my job. To try my own thing, again. After having lived in multiple countries for the past four years. After having started a clothing company in China that failed miserable. After I went back to work a corporate job for two years to fill up my bank account. Again.

I basically quit my job to spread my risk. T diversify my life. And myself. To be less dependent. And more independent. The only person I wanted to depend on was me. And no one else. I only trust myself. And a few other people.

You can't control or predict things. The only thing you can control or predict is the person you see every single morning in the mirror. That's the only person or thing you can control or predict.

Heck, sometimes you don't even have control over yourself. But that's ok. As long as you're trying to improve every single day. I say "try" because most of the time it just doesn't work out. And that's fine, too.

So this is my story. This is the story of how I got to where I am right now.

Where am I right now? Who the hell knows? I don't...

This is the story of a naive little kid who set out to conquer the world. A story that started 7 years ago. A story that probably just got started. A story that will probably never be finished. A story with many ups and downs. Mostly downs.

A story worth telling. A story worth writing down. Mostly for myself, so I don't forget all of these things.

This is the story of how I lost money every single day for more than three years. This is the story about how I lived out of a backpack for the past 7 years.

I'm everywhere and nowhere. And I own nothing and everything.

Intro II -

Why would I have write two intros? I don't know. Why not? That's just the way I roll.

On July 31st I decided to write a book. A month or so earlier, I wrote a blog post called "I'm everywhere and nowhere. And I own nothing and everything.". It was a good post. A post I wanted to write for a long time.

So when I approached someone on Medium (the publishing platform) with a big audience of more than 150,000 followers and asked him if he wanted to feature it he said that I should include around 5-6 images and make it longer.

I added a picture to it and asked him again if he would be able to add it now. Why? Because that's just the way I roll. I'm not quite sure what his response was but it never made it into that publication.

But when I thought about what he said. Why not make it longer? Heck, why not even make a book about it. And that's what I decided to do on July 31st . I decided to write a book based on that one post. By the way you can read that post at the end of the book.

So the idea for this book was born. And on August 1st I started writing that book. And I decided to write one part of it every day for the next 30 days. And at the same time I would publish that one piece of the day on my blog and on Medium.com.

I don't know if anyone has ever done this before. I don't know if anyone has ever written a book in 30 days and then published it on day 31. I don't know if anyone has ever written a book live in front of the whole world.

So that's that. That's the story of this book. That's how I came up with the idea of writing this book. That's how I wrote this book. In just 30 days.

I just did it...

Alright, enough intros for now. Let's get down to business...

I stopped giving a shit a long time ago

We're all going to die.

The one thing that's holding most of us back is that we care way too much about what others think.

What they think about us. What they think about the things we do. What they think about the clothes we wear. The cars we drive. The food we eat. About everything.

We care way too much about what our friends think about us. What our parents think about us. Heck, we even care about what total strangers think about us that we've never met and will probably never meet.

I stopped giving a shit about all of this (and even more) back in 2007. As a matter of fact I probably stopped giving a shit a long time ago. But it wasn't so clear to me back then.

I can still remember what one of my best friends wrote down in my high school graduation yearbook. "He does his own thing." I guess he was right and he knew me a lot better than I knew myself back then.

So some time ago I (consciously or unconsciously) decided to not just live a life. But to create a life.

Here's a funny story...

After I've sent out an email to let people know that I'll be writing a book live in front of the entire world to see and that I'll be writing and publishing one part of that book for the next 30 days, someone sent me an email.

She said that I'm everything she wants to become: Brave. Daring. Enthusiastic. Risk-taking and successful.

I don't think I'm any of this. I just stopped giving a shit. A long time ago. And everything else is just a result of that decision. And when I say this I don't mean hanging out at the beach, drinking beer and partying all night kind of stop giving a shit. No, that's not what I mean at all.

What I mean is that I took the decision of doing whatever I feel like doing and trying out as many different things that might enable me to live the life I truly want to live. Doing the things and living the life that I know deep down inside of me I should be living.

So I'm doing things like writing and publishing one post every single day for the next 30 days and then making a book out of it. That's something I wanted to do and then I just did it. Whatever the consequences. And maybe it will help me get to where I have to be. Maybe it won't. But it doesn't really matter that much.

Many people say that an entrepreneur jumps off a cliff and then finds a way to build a parachute on the way down. This is complete BS. I don't believe in this. At all. It's probably the worst advice ever. 99% of the people will die. If you have no clue about what the hell you're doing you'll probably crash and burn.

So why start with jumping off a cliff? Why not start a bit smaller and less life threatening? Why not start on the trampoline in your back yard?

Look. Most of us just aren't Mark Zuckerberg. Or Steve Jobs. Or Elon Musk. And that's totally fine. Or maybe you are. I don't know you. I'm clearly not.

I think for most of us it's a way better idea to just exercise a bit in the garden on that trampoline before jumping off that cliff. To make many small bets. Before making that huge bet. Instead of jumping off the cliff right away. And once you've mastered that one thing you can go on to the next thing. One step at a time.

So for example, instead of quitting your job without any money in the bank, start something small on the side. Try to make your first few bucks on your own. And then once you see some cash rolling in, go do some more. Go from that trampoline to paragliding.

And once you master that, once you master the first small steps, start working at a company that manufactures parachutes. And once you know how a parachute works and how they're built, you can jump off that cliff. Or you don't. It doesn't matter. What matters is that you don't kill yourself. And jumping off a cliff will most likely kill you when you don't know a thing about parachutes.

Look. Many people talk about doing this or doing that. They talk about writing a book. Many people even say you just need to write 500 or a thousand words a day and at the end of the year you'd have written two or maybe even three books.

And you know what? No one ever does that. People just talk about it. But they never do. It's always easier to just talk about it. Doing is a whole different story. Because you might fail. And people might laugh at you.

And you know what? I don't care about any of this anymore. That's really the only thing that sets me apart. The ONLY thing. If there's something that sets me apart. Because I'm really just an ordinary guy. An ordinary guy who stopped giving a shit a long time ago.

I'm not overly smart. I'm not talented in anything. I've almost failed high school because my essays were so bad. People laughed at me the first time I gave a talk in English in front of a larger crowd. I've written and published more books than I would like to admit. Mostly because none of them was a success.

So how do I do it? How do I keep going? What keeps me alive?

The simple fact that I just don't care anymore.

And I strongly believe that you shouldn't care about all of this stuff either. The one thing you should really care about though, the one thing that really matters is that you do your thing. And be yourself. And start doing the things that will help you live the life you always wanted to live. The life you have to live. No matter what.

And if you don't know what these things are, then think again. You probably know exactly what those things are. It's usually the things you've been trying to ignore. The whole time. These are usually the things you should be doing. The things you were running away from. The things you know deep down you should be doing but were too afraid of.

But without jumping off a cliff. Without killing yourself. Please, don't kill yourself. The world needs you. The world needs to hear your story. So just be patient. And start putting in the work. And try to always get back up again. Go one step at a time. Don't go thirty steps at a time because the only thing that's going to happen is that you're going to stumble and fall. Go one step at a time instead. Because getting back up again after falling down a cliff after you've skipped 30 steps is almost impossible. Not to say deadly.

Look. Life is just a game. And we'll all be dead at the end of it anyway. So you might as well try to live for as long as you can. And try to not kill yourself while at the same time you should try to not live in fear all the time.

Here's a little trick I follow...

I try to constantly remind myself that I won't be able to get out alive of this whole thing anyway. And then I try to remind myself that I don't want to spend my last breaths thinking "what would have happened if I did..."

And instead, I just do it. No matter what. But always try to remember that parachute story. Try to avoid everything stupid. Try to not kill yourself. And go one step at a time.

That's really my entire philosophy. A philosophy that gives me superpowers. The superpower of fearlessness. Of not giving a shit. Because I know I can't lose. Because whatever I do, it won't change the simple fact that after 80 or so years I'll be dead anyway.

Is this a depressing thought?

For some people it is. For me it isn't. For me it is the fuel that keeps me going. It is the air I breathe that keeps me alive. It is the food I eat to be able to keep moving.

It's about time.

It's about time to stop giving a shit.

So you can finally start creating your own...

I had the chance to save the world. But I blew it.

I didn't want to start working. I was freaking out...

It was 2009. I was 25 years old and I had no clue about what to do next. I was studying something that I was barely interested in, just to keep as many doors open as possible.

I had no clue about what I wanted to do with my life. So I thought keeping as many doors open as possible might be the best choice.

To this date I don't know if that's true. But when I take a look at what I'm doing now, it might really have been the best choice. At least for me.

I studied business so I could literally become everything and nothing at the same time. Nothing was really tangible. Everything was highly theoretical and I didn't really have any practical skills. I wasn't really able to do anything. I felt like a total fraud.

But what I didn't know back then is that 99% of the people with a university degree aren't really able to create or do anything. Back then I didn't know that we're all part of a big fat ponzi scheme built on power point slides, business jibber jabber and other things that no one really understands.

And at the end of the day you'll become the manager of everything and everyone just because you're constantly talking about stuff no one really understands and people assume that you must be smart and know what you're talking about. When in reality no one has any clue about anything they're talking about. Including me. Especially me...

Don't believe this is true? You don't have to. Here's a little story. Here's the story about how I predicted the financial crisis in 2008. Or could have. But I didn't...

Back in 2008 I attended a class that was called futures and options. It was about a lot of stock market mumbo jumbo that doesn't really help anybody. And one day there was a guy from Lehman Brothers coming into class and he gave a guest lecture. They do this from time to time when they're looking for interns. So for about two hours I saw hundreds of graphs and hundreds of lines going from left to right. From right to left. From the top to the bottom. And I didn't understand a damn thing.

And I'm sure the guy explaining it didn't understand a damn thing either. And once those two hours were over, the guy finished up saying "and this is how we guarantee our customers a 100% safe return of 10%."

And I was like, "how the heck is that even possible? This can not work! This is a total scam."

Ok, I never said that out loud. But I told my classmates that I didn't understand a damn thing what this guy was even talking about for the past two hours. I said this can't be possible. Maybe it really is possible. I don't know. I almost failed that course.

And the only thing that I can remember from that course is that everything this guy said didn't make any sense to me at all and that Lehman Brothers went out of business a few months later. So that was that.

I had the chance to save the world. But I blew it...

Still, I had no clue about what I wanted to do with my life. I was scared. I was scared about making the wrong decisions. Just a short year before my graduation I had thousands of thoughts racing through my head. Thoughts like..

What if I end up at a job that I don't like? What if I'll be stuck there for the rest of my life? What if I get depressed? What if..? What if..? What if..? Aaaaaaah!

All of these thoughts were killing me. I was scared of the future. I was scared that I would never be able to support myself. Layoffs everywhere. How will I ever be able to find a job that I like that pays enough to feed me and my future family and my unborn kids?

So I did everything a sane person would do in such a situation...

I just walked away. I left the country. And went to China. As an exchange student. Not because I thought China is the new promised land or because I wanted to learn Chinese. No, not at all. I went to China because I always wanted to go to Japan.

Doesn't make any sense? It sure doesn't. Nothing makes any sense when we look at it right now. It only makes sense in retrospect. When we're able to put all the pieces together. When we're able to put all our puzzle pieces together and they form a beautiful picture.

Alright. The reason why I didn't go to Japan is a little less philosophic. It's just that at that year when I wanted to go to Japan my university didn't have any exchange program going on with Japan. So the only choices that were left were Israel, Russia or China. And because I had no clue about anything back then (and still don't), I thought China is as close to Japan as it gets. So that was that.

I went to study in China for a semester. And that semester turned into almost two years. And it lead to me starting a company in China and miserably failing at it. As well as a short side career as an English teacher at a Chinese and a Japanese company. And to me learning a bit of Chinese. A tiny little bit.

Oh yeah. And I finally learned something tangible. I learned how to use illustrator to design t-shirts, how to screen print and how to use a sewing machine. Not because I thought it was a lot of fun. It was out of necessity and a lack of cash. And because of one of the most important lessons that I had to learn the hard way doing business in China. A rule that probably applies to making business everywhere.

You can only rely on yourself. And no one else...

Look. All of this didn't help me to change the world. It didn't do much. But it was one piece of my puzzle. A piece that would lead to many more seemingly unrelated pieces that would ultimately lead me to the stuff I do right now.

What is it that I do now?

I don't know. I'm still busy collecting pieces.

I'm busy collecting pieces of my puzzle that might maybe one day form a beautiful picture that might maybe change the world and portray one of the most beautiful pictures the entire world has ever seen.

A picture we're all capable of painting. A picture that needs courage. A picture that needs patience. A picture that needs confidence. And faith.

A picture of a life well lived...

The thing that helped me to go from just living a life to creating a life

A while ago someone asked me if one of my books was available as PDF. He wanted to read it on his tablet. I realized that I didn't offer it as PDF. Stupid me!

He told me he's currently on a sabbatical, traveling the world and thinking about what he could do next in life.

He said he was trying to think about what work he could do so that when he wakes up every single morning he'd feel energized.

He was trying to figure out what would make him smile every single morning.

But he couldn't figure it out. There are just way too many things going through his head. Too many things to think about. To worry about. And not enough time. Never enough time! Arghhh!

I think that's a problem many people have. A problem that I had myself for a long time, too. A problem I still have every once in a while. And I strongly believe that the only way to solve this riddle, to solve your riddle, to solve my riddle, to solve all our riddles is to stop thinking.

Constantly thinking about things won't do anything. You will never find a solution just by thinking about it. Especially when it comes to something complex like finding your passion. Finding your calling. Or finding something you might enjoy doing. Something that makes you smile when you get up every single morning.

The simple truth is this…

We don't know what we enjoy doing, what our calling or our passion is, what we should be doing, simply because we stopped trying. We stopped experimenting. We stopped searching. And most importantly we stopped doing.

Some time in our early twenties or maybe even earlier we stop experimenting. Because everybody tells us that we need to know what we want to do with our lives. "You have to be something. Or someone." is what everybody tells us.

But the truth is that no one is able to know what to do for the rest of their lives at that age. At any age as a matter of fact.

Now in my thirties, I start to realize that you will never really know what you'd want to do for the rest of your life. Simply because the rest of your life is a hell lot of time. And you know what? That's totally fine.

What's not so fine though is the fact that we were and are being pushed into a system, into a way of thinking that kills pretty much everything that defines most of us. It kills the explorer. The hunter. The gatherer.

A system that wants us to choose what we want to do for the rest of our lives. When our lives have barely even started yet. It's just impossible.

So instead of continuing to explore, we settle. We settle for the things society and people expect from us. And then somewhere along the way some of us, not necessarily all of us, get stuck.

And some of us just don't know what they'd love to do so they'd be able wake up in the morning with a smile on their faces. Some of us need more time to explore. Not more time to think. But more time to do.

And I think that's the only way out. You need to give yourself some time. Some time to try things out. To test new things. To figure out what you enjoy doing. And getting away from all the thinking.

Too much thinking never solves anything. Only doing does. And thinking every once in a while about what you're currently doing, what you might have done wrong and what you could do to improve what you're doing might also help.

Look. You can think about things for years and years and years. But if you never do anything, then you'll still be stuck at the exact same spot you've already been a few years ago.

Just like they say, it's your best thinking that got you here.

And the one thing that's responsible for all the thinking, for all the fear based decision making, for making all the decisions that ultimately hold us back from doing, from experimenting and experiencing life is the so called lizard brain.

That part of the brain that's responsible for our survival instinct. It's been there for tens of thousands of years. Maybe even more. I'm no expert. But today, we call it the amygdala.

Even though we gave it a new name, it's still pretty much useless these days and only holds us back from living the life we truly want to live. The life we deserve to live. To be able to tap into our strengths and to unleash our potential.

The lizard brain has been responsible for our survival for the past tens of thousands of years. It's an instinct guided part of the brain that starts to kick in whenever we are in a potentially dangerous or life threatening situation.

And back in the days when we were still cavemen and cavewomen pretty much everything was life threatening with all the wild animals out there. So we really needed it. But today, not so much anymore.

Back in the days we needed it because whenever there was the tiniest bit of uncertainty about what that sound back there in those bushes could have been, it pushed us to run away. After all, that sound could have been a tiger. Or any other large animal that wants to eat us.

But today, most situations aren't so life threatening anymore. But it still operates like this. And to increase its chances of survival that lizard brain still wants us to avoid every situation that's even just a tiny little bit filled with uncertainty. It feeds on certainty. And craves safety. And that's why we're always shooting for the safe thing. Because the lizard brain is playing its trick on us. It wants to survive. It wants us to think about the negative part of everything. To protect itself.

And the only way I've ever been able to tame my lizard brain was by doing what I like to call "the grandpa test." It has helped me over and over again to get the lizard brain to shut up and get going. It has helped me to stay focused on my end goal. Over and over again.

And the first time I used it was when I decided to go to China, instead of looking for a job like all my fellow classmates did back in 2009. It didn't make a lot of sense back then and I wasn't sure if it was the right decision. Some part of me said I should be reasonable and look for a job. It was probably the lizard brain trying to protect itself.

I don't know how I came up with the grandpa test back then. I certainly did not read about it in a book. Simply because I read less than 10 books in total back in my first 27 years of living on this planet. So it must have been something else. Anyways.

So here's how the grandpa test goes...

In every situation I find myself in and am in doubt about whether or not I should do something, I imagine my 80 year old self sitting on my veranda (or the street corner, who knows?) reflecting about my life. About all of the things I've done. And all of the things I didn't do.

And if that thing I'm currently not sure about doing is something where my future 80 year old self might ask himself "How would my life have looked like if I did it? Would it be any different?", then I just do it.

Simply because I don't want to look back on a life full of regrets. A life where I didn't do many potentially life changing things, just because I couldn't get that damn lizard brain to shut up.

Look. I don't know if this is a good way of living life. I don't know if it will work for you. Maybe it will. Maybe it won't. But it worked for me. Over and over again. And that's really all I do to get going. Over and over again. That's all I do tame and fight my lizard brain. To do the things I'm scared of doing.

And that's what got me to China and ultimately to where I am right now.

That's how I went from just living a life to creating my own life...

Nothing really matters. Until it does.

He was spitting all over the place while he was trying to talk. He couldn't talk properly anymore. I couldn't understand a single word he was saying. And then I just left the dinner and went home.

I went home to the flat where I lived with four other people. During those two years in China I probably lived together with 20 different people or so. In 3 different places. Maybe even more. So I went home and one of my room mates was smoking a joint. He was some sort of drug dealer before.

I gave it a try. But I never really feel anything. The only thing that happens is that I get sleepy. So I went to bed. And the next day I walked two hours across the whole city to eat one of the best burgers I've ever had in my entire life. The burger place was called Munchies. So now that I think about it, maybe it did have an effect on me...

I was at that dinner the other day because I was invited to have dinner with the family of one of my students who I taught English for a while. Yes, I also taught English for a while. And yes I'm not an English native speaker. And yes, it didn't make any sense at all back then.

The dinner was really great until her husband got a pretty fancy looking bottle with alcohol in it out of somewhere. It was Baijiu. That's some sort of Chinese rice alcohol. It basically tastes like gasoline. Probably even worse.

But this one was quite different. It was actually really good. He told me that you can't buy this one in any store. It's a special kind that's reserved for politicians or something like that. I don't know if that was true. But that's what he said. He had a business and was doing something with the government. So it could be true.

Long story short. He got pretty drunk. Luckily, I didn't. And we talked about all sorts of stuff before I wasn't able to understand him anymore. We also talked about Chinese zodiac signs. He told me that he was born in the year of the dragon. And that I was born in the year of the rat.

I liked that.

Sometimes I really feel like a rat. I can survive pretty much everywhere and get used to pretty much everything really fast. I don't need a lot to survive. Just the basics. Just like a rat. So maybe all of this zodiac sign stuff does make sense after all.

I really don't know why I even started teaching English in China. I'm not even a native speaker. It didn't make any sense at all. Just like starting a clothing brand in China for the Chinese market without having any clue about clothing or being able to speak Chinese. None of it didn't make any sense at all. But that didn't really matter that much. Nothing really matters.

One day a guy at school asked me if I wanted to teach English. I said sure, why not. But I'm not a native speaker. And he said that it doesn't really matter. He'll just tell the agency that I'm from Canada. I said I'm in. Looking back, maybe he didn't think I would say yes. And why would I? I really don't know. But I just did.

So I started teaching some English on the side while trying to finish my master's degree, while trying to start a business and trying to learn Chinese. All at the same time. Not surprisingly, none of these things really worked out. But that didn't really matter that much either.

Oh and by the way, please don't tell anyone about this. Because I might end up in jail. And I don't want to go to jail in China. Maybe they're already looking for me. I have no clue. So please, don't tell anyone about this.

What I think matters though is that you use your twenties or thirties, heck maybe even your entire life to do things. To experiment. To try as many different things as possible. To not get stuck along the way. To do as many things as possible that don't seem to make any sense at all. Just because right now nothing makes any sense at all. Nothing really makes sense when you're trying to predict the future. It only makes sense in retrospect.

I don't think your twenties, heck your entire life is there for winning trophies. For perfecting your CV or anything like that. Or maybe it is. I don't know. I did all of it, too. But didn't really end up using any of it. Nonetheless, it's always good to have a backup plan.

What I think it's all about at the end of the day is to collect as many different pieces of your puzzle as possible. A puzzle you have no clue about how it's going to look like once it's one. Maybe it will look like the Eiffel Tower? Maybe it will look like the Great Wall? Who knows? No one knows...

And when you're collecting pieces for an unknown puzzle it really is all about saying "yes" more often than saying "no". Especially when you're starting off. Especially when you're young. To make sure that some of the pieces you picked up along the way match your final puzzle.

Sure, some people are geniuses and get everything right the very first time. Some people end up marrying their high school love. Some people end up starting Facebook.

But most of us just don't. We need to collect more pieces. We need more time. More time to find our own personal Facebook. More time to find our high school love.

Here's the thing...

When you're trying to predict the future, nothing will really make any sense.

Nothing will really fit the puzzle you have in your head.

But what if the puzzle in your head isn't your puzzle? What if your puzzle doesn't even look anything like the puzzle you imagined? Think about it...

All of this stuff only makes sense in retrospect.

And not when you look at it right now.

That's why nothing really matters.

Until it does...

About that one time I started a company in China

I never thought about starting a company. I never thought about going to China. And not even in my wildest dreams would I have thought that I would end up starting a company in China. But that's exactly what happened.

It just happened...

Back in 2009 I didn't even know what a startup was. I had no clue about anything. But I liked the thought of not having to go back to Germany because I didn't want to start looking for a job. So starting a business seemed like a great idea.

It was a total coincidence and not planned at all. Most of the good things in life just happen. Most of the good things can't be planned and are usually a total coincidence. And most of the things you try to plan and map out usually turn into something horrible. Or into things that don't work out.

That has at least been the case for me pretty much all the time. For pretty much everything. So I stopped planning.

Here's the thing...

To me it seems that most people wait for that perfect set of cards to go all in. Most people wait for that one big idea. That one big master plan. That one person who's going to save them. But this never really happens. This only happens in Hollywood.

That perfect hand to go all in will never come. Because that perfect hand doesn't really exist.

That one big idea will never come. Because that one big idea is the result of many small ideas.

That big master plan will never come. Because that big master plan doesn't really exist.

Just like no one is ever going to save you. Because only you can.

Most things in life are a coincidence. Most of the hands you're played are not worth playing. Still, you've gotta try to make the best out of every hand you get. No matter how good or bad.

And it all start with a first small step. When you take a step without really knowing what could happen next. When everything and nothing is possible.

Even me writing this right here is a total coincidence. I never planned any of this.

It's a coincidence that started when I first met my business partner in China in 2009. We totally randomly met in a hostel in Shanghai. And it turned out that we were in the same exchange program. And then it turned out that we were in similar courses.

And then one thing lead to another and boom! two years later I was almost broke and had to go back home to Germany to find a job to fill up my bank account.

And it all started with a first step. Without really knowing what could happen next. Everything and nothing was possible. And without that first step I wouldn't be writing this and you wouldn't be reading this.

And that's the magic of it. Of what? Of life!

And then again, when I came back to Germany one thing led to another and I ended up working in venture capital for a bit in Berlin and then in New York. Until I decided to quit my job. And then I wrote a book about it.

And because that book wasn't a success and I didn't have a job anymore and every time I checked my bank account the numbers were getting smaller and smaller, I knew I had to come up with some more ideas. And then some more.

Until all of this somehow led me to writing 7 books and more than 500 blog posts and publishing one part of a book for 30 days and releasing it on day 31.

Everything started with that initial coincidence. It all started with that one step that could mean nothing and everything. That one step that led to everything.

So what's my point here?

I guess there is no point. There are just coincidences. And how you play the set of cards that's handed to you. No matter how good or bad. It's also about recognizing and grabbing opportunities when they show up. Instead of hunting them down. Because what happens when you want something so badly that it hurts is that you're going to end up nowhere.

It's like the universe and everybody around you can feel your desperation. It's like they can smell it. And in our world, no one really wants to deal with someone who's desperate.

And that's the story about that one time I started a company in China.

How one coincidence led to another.

And how one step led to many more steps...

It's time for me to quit...

I lived in China on and off for almost two years trying to build that company.

And what I had to realize back then is that quitting is hard. Really, really hard. It's a lot harder than starting. Knowing when to quit is probably the hardest thing out there.

Admitting failure, even if it's just temporary, even if you've learned a hell lot is never easy. It's one of the toughest things out there. Telling yourself "Yupp, that's it, I'll have to pack my things and leave" is a lot harder than it sounds.

So here are a few things I've learned back then. And over the following years. Here are the things that made me realize that it was about time to pack my things and go. Over and over again...

a) GETTING SICK

When you're constantly sick, getting sick or jumping from one sickness to the next, then your body wants to send you a message. It's your body telling you that it's time to stop. That it's not worth it. That you should be doing something else. And when that happens then you know that it's probably a good idea to pack your things and go. Health is more important than anything else.

Because what's going to happen when you're constantly sick, when you don't get enough sleep, is that everything else will stop working. You won't be able to think straight anymore. You'll constantly be making the wrong decisions and most importantly you'll stop seeing clearly. And from there everything will get worse and worse.

I was constantly sick. My body was constantly sending me signals. And I tried to ignore them for as long as I could. One time when I went back home to Germany some of my friends told me that my face was yellow. That's how sick I was. And that's when I knew that I had to get the hell out of there. That I had to pack my stuff and leave...

b) EATING JUNK FOOD

When you're constantly eating junk food and drinking unhealthy soft drinks it's your body trying to send you a signal. Heck! Again? What's up with all of these signals?

Your body wants to tell you that something is wrong. That something is missing. And whatever that is, your body wants that feeling to go away. Your body doesn't want to feel bad, so just like a drug addict, your body is telling you to inject as much trash into your body as possible so you can feel a bit better for a bit.

But after that quick high it will be even worse than before. It's a vicious circle. A circle you need to break out of as fast as you can. The sooner the better...

c) DRINKING ALCOHOL

Here's why most people go out and party like crazy and get drunk on the weekends. Or as a matter of fact buy all sorts of crap they don't really need.

People do it because they tell themselves that they deserve it. That all week long they've been doing things they didn't enjoy doing. Things that didn't make them happy.

"Screw this. Now is "me time". Now is the time to be happy and pack all the fun that was missing during the week into a few short hours. Let's get all the fun and happiness from that week back."

What people don't realize is that every time you get super drunk, you're pretty much stealing happiness from the next day. Or the following day. And depending on how often you do this, you might end up stealing all of your life's happiness. Only to end up being an unhappy shell of what you've once been...

d) EVERYTHING

Alright. Alright. Here's something more positive. Another sign that it might be a good time to quit is that you've done everything you can. And I don't mean that you've tried hiring people to do the job for you but couldn't find anyone to do it for you.

What I mean with doing everything you can is to literally do everything you can. And not hire other people to do it for you. And not to just drop it if you don't have enough money to hire someone to do it for you. No, I mean that you'd have to learn and then do everything yourself. And if that fails, then move on...

When we couldn't find a designer because everyone was charging us a ridiculous amount of money, I started learning Illustrator and started designing t-shirts. And then I designed all our products.

When we couldn't find a factory to produce in small quantities, I went out there and learned everything about screen printing and printed the shirts myself.

I also learned how to use a sewing machine to sew the tags on the shirts. So if you've done everything you can and it still doesn't work out then just pack your things and leave...

e) FUN

When it's just no fun anymore at all, then just quit. Life is too short to do things that aren't fun anymore. But try to remember d)...

f) LEARNING

If you feel like you don't or can't learn anything anymore because you've already learned everything you can and don't see how you could progress any further, then just quit.

Too many people get stuck in dead end jobs, projects, relationships or whatever because at one point they stopped progressing. And then lost all of their momentum. And losing momentum is the worst thing that could ever happen to you.

When you're standing still for just a few short days, weeks, months or even worse a few years, then you'll almost never be able to get that momentum back. It's super hard to get momentum back going. It's not impossible. But very, very hard.

That's why so many talented and smart people get stuck in life and end up in dead end jobs. They've missed the point of moving on to the next thing. They've lost their momentum.

Never lose momentum! And when you start losing momentum, you have to get out of there as fast as possible...

g) EXERCISE

At my first job I usually came home around 5 or 6pm. Sometimes even 4pm. But still, I felt so tired every day I came home it was insane. I felt like I ran a marathon. I couldn't do anything anymore when I came home. All I could do was to turn on the TV. Only to wake up at 3am in the morning with my work clothes still on. When you're constantly doing things you don't really want to be doing, you'll always feel exhausted. It's your body telling you that you should quit...

h) OPPORTUNITIES

As soon as a better opportunity comes along, take it. It doesn't make any sense to keep doing that other thing when all you secretly want is to to that new thing. That thing that might be better for you. And everybody else around you.

But what about loyalty? There's nothing more loyal than leaving or quitting when you get a better opportunity. Because when you stay you'll only destroy other people's opportunities. Be it in a relationship, a business or whatever.

If you want to take that opportunity but you don't take it, you'll only feel miserable and make everyone else around you feel miserable as well. Not only this. You'll also be constantly thinking about that other thing. Which will in the mid to long term hurt your performance...

i) SLEEP

If you don't sleep enough your mind will always be weak. And when your mind is weak you'll constantly be eating junk food or drinking brown sugar water. Or alcohol. You need to be well rested to be able to resist all the temptations out there.

Again, it's a vicious circle. If you're not able to get enough sleep for a period longer than you'd like to admit to your friends or your family then get the hell out of there...

But even more importantly when you start to realize that the things you're doing don't really have an impact, that no one really needs what you're doing, that someone else could easily be doing the exact same thing you're doing, when you realize that you're easily replaceable, then just pack your things and leave.

Because what that means is that you're not doing what you're supposed to be doing. That you're not doing that one thing you were sent here to be doing. That one thing only you can do.

And you need to do everything you can to do the thing you were sent here for. You owe it to yourself. And the people around you. Heck, you owe it to the entire world. So get going...

Building someone else's dream is totally fine (for a while)

You don't always have to be building and working on your own dreams.

As a matter of fact I didn't even know until I was 28 what my dream was. Even right now I'm not sure what exactly it is that I want to do for the rest of my life. I don't really know what I was sent here for. And that's totally fine.

Right now I enjoy writing. Tomorrow I might enjoy teaching. And then maybe next year I might enjoy doing something else. Who knows? Everything around us is changing so fast. And so are we.

Over the past seven years I've gone from entrepreneur to employee, from employee to author, from author to entrepreneur and then from entrepreneur to blogger, author and I don't like to admit it, but I somehow also got into digital marketing. And who knows, maybe next year I'll take on a job. Who knows?

Nothing is forever...

And when I got started with all of this, the first thing I ever worked on was building someone else's dream.

Simply because I didn't have any dreams. It's not that I wasn't ambitious or didn't have any goals in life. It's just that I had absolutely no clue what I wanted to do.

And sometimes it's not about knowing what you want to do. Sometimes it's about waiting, getting ready and grabbing opportunities instead.

So the only thing I really knew back then was that I didn't want to start working a full time job. I didn't want to be stuck in a cubicle for the rest of my life.

So I grabbed the opportunity and joined my partner and helped him build his dream. The kind of business he wanted to build. It wasn't necessarily the kind of business I wanted to start or to build.

But you know what?

Looking back, this might have been the best decision I've ever made in my entire life.

Not only did I learn a hell lot from him, but it's also the main reason why I'm doing what I'm doing now. If I didn't join him I would probably not be sitting here and writing these lines. And instead I would probably be sitting somewhere in a cubicle.

Which, by the way happened right after we had to shutdown that company. Which, by the way might have been the second best thing that ever happened to me. Working a corporate job for almost two years taught me more than I'd like to admit.

And I'm very grateful for every teacher and real life lesson I learned in those two years. It helped me to understand how big companies really work. But even more importantly I learned a lot about how people think and the psychology behind the smallest things out there.

And without both of these experiences I would probably not be where I am right now. And in both situations I worked on building someone else's dreams. So I think building someone else's dream isn't that bad after all.

Sometimes it's not about working on your dreams. Sometimes it's about working on someone else's dreams. To get you ready for your own dreams. To observe, see and learn.

I guess what I'm trying to say is that it's not such a bad idea to put your dreams on hold for a while. It's not such a bad idea to work on building and making other people's dreams come true first. Because then you'd know how to build your own dreams.

When you're working for someone else, when you're working on making someone else's dreams come true, you're basically getting paid for learning. You're getting paid for learning how to make your own dreams come true.

Which to me sounds like a pretty good deal.

And once you've learned enough you can go on and start working on your own dreams. Either on your own or with the support of the person or the organization whose dreams you were working on before.

Building someone else's dream is fine as long as you see it as what it is. As an opportunity to learn what it takes to make your own dreams come true.

But try to make sure you don't get too comfortable building other people's dreams. Because sometimes that safety net might turn out to be a spider web with a big fat spider on it waiting to suck all the life out of you...

Everybody was laughing at me

Everybody says that you've gotta know your strengths. You've gotta know who you are. And you've gotta be authentic. Talk and write in your own voice. That's what they all say.

But how the heck do you even know what your strengths are? How do you find your strengths? How do you speak in your own voice when you constantly feel like you don't even have a voice at all? When you constantly feel like you're just not good enough.

Look. Here's something most people won't tell you. To find your strengths, to find your own true voice, to figure out who you really are deep down, you've gotta take a look at your weaknesses first. And not your strengths. I strongly believe that to be able to find your strengths you've gotta look at your weaknesses first.

Here's the thing about your strengths. About the things you're already good at. Well, you're already good at it so there's no real need to put in a lot of work to improve. And that's the problem. Because you're already good at it your learning curve will be very flat. Simply because when you're already good at something you've gotta put in a hell lot of work to get just a tiny little bit better at it.

So you'll never be able to build up momentum. And without momentum everything is a thousand times harder. When you're already naturally good at something the effort to reach the next level seems to outweigh the potential benefits. Also, when you're already good at something you feel like you know everything already and don't need to put in more work. And when I say you, I'm basically talking about myself.

I was always pretty good in sports. I was always one of the best in my class. But I never really continued any of it. Simply because I thought I was already good enough. And I thought I didn't need to learn more about techniques, training programs and so on. The needed effort to improve seemed to outsize the results. By far. The learning curve would have been pretty flat. Building momentum to keep going would have been just too damn hard. So I never really continued doing sports when I got older.

On the other hand, if you take a look at your weaknesses it's a whole different story. It's so much easier to build up momentum, to see first results and the learning curve in general is a lot steeper. As long as you're understanding, accepting ad embracing one simple thing.

No one is good at anything when they start. We all suck when we start something new. Your first 100 blog posts will suck. Your first 50 YouTube videos will suck. Your first 20 talks in public will suck. Your first 10 books will suck. It is what it is. And that's totally fine.

As long as you keep putting in the work. As long as you keep pushing. As long as you see skills as what they are. They are build over time. They don't have anything to do with talent. Skills are the result of hard work, persistence and resilience. And never giving up. No matter what.

Most of the people you see at the top right now, no matter what area in life we're talking about, started from the exact same spot you are right now. Where I am right now. They started from the bottom. And worked their way to the top. And that's how they found their strengths. Tapped into them and unleashed their potential. That's how they found their own unique voice. By putting in the work first.

So if you don't know what your strengths are, if you don't know who you are or what you stand for, then take a look at your weaknesses. In many cases these things aren't even real weaknesses. Mostly, it's just people telling you that you're not good at it. Your teacher, society, your friends, your family, heck the entire world.

But you know what? You teacher, society, your friends, your family and the entire world, they all believe in the concept of talent. They all believe that to be good at something you need a god given talent. And this is BS. There's no such thing as talent. There's only putting in the work. And building skills over time. By doing. And not by talking.

And that's why all of these people will tell you that you don't have what it takes. And when you've heard it often enough you'll believe what they say. And what's going to happen then is that you don't even try to put in the work it would take to become better at something you might maybe enjoy doing.

Look. There are no talented singers. There are only singers who put in the work for many, many years and singers who didn't.

There are no talented writers. There are only writers who put in the work for many, many years and writers who didn't.

There are no talented artists. Or designers. There are only artists and designers who put in the work for many, many years and the ones who didn't.

Sure, you might say that you need to be tall to become a professional NBA basketball player or something else where it's primarily about physique.

And you know what?

You might be right. But that's a whole different story. Because we're talking about physique here. Being tall is almost like a requirement to become a professional basketball player. But that doesn't mean that every tall person will automatically be a professional basketball player.

They might have an advantage, but they'd still have to put in the work. Probably even more so than anyone else. Simply because when you're taller than the average person then it's a lot more likely that you're going to have problems with your back or have some other problems related to your physique. Simply because our bodies and the world are made for shorter people.

On another note. Height isn't a necessity to become a professional NBA player either. Muggsy Bogues, who is only 1,6m (5ft 3) tall played very successfully in the NBA for 15 seasons. He put in the work. Maybe even more so than anybody else probably. He turned his weakness into his own unique strength.

Let's take a look at some of the folks out there who are rightfully preaching that you need to find your strengths to be able to unleash your potential. It's always interesting to see how they started. Just take a look at Gary Vaynerchuk's first videos on YouTube. They were very, very different from what he's doing now.

I'm not saying they were bad. But they were also not very good compared to what he's doing now. They were just ok. He didn't seem very talented. He also didn't seem to have any special skills. He seemed like a totally regular guy who made a bunch of videos. A regular guy just like you and me who put in the work over many, many years.

What got him to do be able to do the mind blowing type of videos he's doing today is that he consistently put in the work. He has probably done more than 1000 videos before he got this good. Heck maybe even 2000 videos. And the same golds true for his talks. He has probably given a few hundred talks already.

Or the Beatles who played thousands of shows in shitty clubs in Hamburg before they became famous. Or Bill Gates who had access to computers before anybody else had. They put in the work first. And that's their biggest competitive advantage. When they appeared on stage, when they appeared in the spotlight, they already had thousands of hours of training.

And that's what people tend to forget. When you see someone or start using something that you have never heard of before, that something or that someone already went through years and years of hustling. Of putting in the work. Of getting better every single day. Of improving features. Or what not.

And the moment you see those things, the moment they hit the spotlight and you start using these things or start following these people, the really hard work was already done.

So it might look like overnight success. Or god given talent. When in reality it's the result of years and years of putting in more work than anybody else.

Just like Pokemon Go was a huge success when it first came out. It looks like an overnight. But when you look close enough you'll realize that it was a story in the making for many, many years.

The folks who did Pokemon Go were working for Google for many, many years. They were even part of the team building Google Maps. So what you looks like an overnight success is really the result of years and years of engineering experience and knowledge from some of the most talented engineers from one of the most successful companies in the world.

And that's why I think when you're trying to find your strengths and your true voice you'd have to take a look at your weaknesses first. The things you're not so good at, yet. The things you can can still improve rather easily and build up momentum to then be able to carry that momentum further to get past the roadblocks you'll encounter along the way.

Let me tell you a story here real quick. Well, actually two stories. And it won't actually be quick...

The first time I gave a talk in front of a larger crowd of more than 40 people or so everybody started laughing when it was my turn. It was so humiliating. And I had no clue what was going on. Nobody wanted to tell me what was going on. Not even the people I was presenting with wanted to tell me.

So after a few minutes the laughing stopped. Those few minutes might have been some of the worst few minutes of my entire life. I thought I peed myself or something like that but couldn't find any evidence anywhere.

As you might imagine, I never wanted to give a talk ever again for the rest of my life.

And it took me more than five years before I gave a talk in front of a larger crowd again. And that was a talk in front of a crowd of more than 120 people. It was the first stop of a speaking tour I organized myself for myself in 2013 with 10 talks or so.

I was scared of doing it. But I knew that this would be the only way that I would ever get over my fear and turn my "weakness" into a strength.

In case you're wondering what happened back in 2008 when everybody was laughing at me, here's what happened...

I basically said the exact same thing the guy before me said. I was so nervous that I didn't even pay attention to what he said. Or what I had to say. That's how nervous I was.

It was a group presentation and because I designed the whole presentation for the entire group I was familiar with the entire content. So that was that. Looking back, I have to admit that it was pretty funny and I would probably also have laughed. A lot.

And since 2013 I gave more than 30 talks. I have been invited to speak at dozens of conferences. I was mentoring at dozens of events for hundreds of young entrepreneurs. I guess it turned out ok. And you know what? I really enjoy giving talks now. And people have even paid me a few times to give talks.

Even though, no, probably because so many people laughed at me the very first time I gave a talk in front of a larger crowd...

When I was in high school I almost failed 10th class because my writing was so bad. I constantly got Ds, Es and sometimes even Fs on my essays. I was one of the worst students in my class.

And you know what? I was really bad. It wasn't the teacher's fault. It was all my fault. How do I know? Because not too long ago I found an essay I wrote in high school. And it was horrible. I deserved every bad grade I ever got.

And the reason why I was so bad was very simple. I never read books until I was 28. I never put in the work. And now just a few short years later you're reading one of my essays online. In just a few short years I was able to build an audience online I would never have thought would even be possible in my wildest dreams.

And I got to where I am now simply because I started putting in the work. Because I thought that writing might be something I might maybe enjoy doing. And then I just did it. And never really stopped for the past three years. And for the past year or so I've written and published one article a day. Because if you want to get better at something you like, you've gotta put in more work than anybody else.

I also published 7 books in those 3 years. This is the eighth. Sure, none of the 7 books was a huge success. But every book I write, every article I write gets me closer to it. And every article you write, every book you publish will get you closer to it.

Every painting you paint gets you closer to it. Every talk you give gets you closer to it. Every email you write gets you closer to it. Every date you go on gets you closer to it.

Closer to what?

Closer to the life you want to live.

To the life you have to live.

To the life you deserve to live...

Nothing lasts forever

Over the past 7 years I went from being an entrepreneur to employee, from employee to author and then to blogger and public speaker and then back to being an entrepreneur.

So what do I do now?

I don't really know. I now do all of the above things at the same time. And when new people I meet ask me what I'm doing I usually just tell them that I do Internet stuff. For most people that's enough. Because most people don't know a lot about Internet stuff.

I don't know what I'm going to do next year. Maybe I'll start working at a company. I really enjoy all of this digital marketing stuff that I've started doing recently. It's pretty much the backbone of everything.

So my point is this...

Nothing lasts forever. Today is today. And tomorrow is a new day. And tomorrow you could already be doing something else entirely. Something you'd never even thought possible in your wildest dreams.

Sure, it doesn't happen just like that. You need to constantly be creating opportunities for yourself and the people around you. And maybe one day one of the seeds you planted grows into a strong enough tree. Into an opportunity worth taking a closer look at.

But to me it seems that lot of people think that if they take that one job that their life is over. That they'll have to work at that company for the rest of their life.

Or when they quit their jobs, start their own thing and for some reason it doesn't work out that they're doomed for life. That they'll never ever find a job ever again. That they'll be unemployable. That they'd have to live on the streets.

I think this is BS. A a matter of fact if you've started something on your own, if you've created something out of nothing then you'd become a lot more valuable for most companies out there.

Simply because most people have never created something out of nothing. Most people have no clue about how to create something out of nothing.

In the land of the blind, the one-eyed man is king.

And the more things you have to show, the more things you've created, the less people will care about your CV. Or what you've done in the past.

Here's something that many people underestimate...

The skills you learn when you're out on your own are all marketable skills. Skills that will help you get a job. They'll expose you to even more opportunities. Simply because most people out there don't have any skills at all. I didn't have any tangible skills when I started three years ago, either.

And now I know quite a lot about digital marketing (real hands on stuff, not some fluffy strategic stuff), copy writing, building an audience and many more things. And these are all valuable and marketable skills. Skills that will set you apart.

Sure, some companies won't hire people who've failed when they were out on their own. But these are the companies you wouldn't want to work at anyway. If you work for or with small minded people, you'll become small minded yourself.

Look. More and more incumbents and large corporations are craving to find people they now call intrapreneurs. People who do the same stuff that entrepreneurs do. Just in a much safe environment than being out alone in the dark all by yourself.

And you know who they'd love to hire? Former entrepreneurs. Because incumbents and all these old companies are struggling to generate enough revenues. Their revenues are going down. Instead of up.

I know. It can be scary. And I thought the exact same thing.

When I moved back to Germany after my company failed I thought I was unemployable. I thought I had the word failure written all over my face. I thought it was over. But I needed a job. Very badly. Simply because I burned through a lot of cash. And needed to fill up my bank account. For my next thing.

So when I came back home I sent out 5 or 6 CVs. And within just two short weeks I got a job offer. And I took that offer. And worked at that company for almost two years. And learned a hell lot of stuff about how corporations work.

And I think the only reason they hired me back then was because of what I did in the past. Because I created something out of nothing. Because I was the one-eyed man in the land of the blind. And not because of which school I went to.

And then two years later I quit my job. I thought that I had seen and learned enough. So it turns out that I was unemployable. But not because no one wanted to hire me. But because I didn't want to work for someone else anymore.

Nothing lasts forever...

"You will regret this"

He told me that I will regret this for the rest of my life. That I did a very big mistake.

I don't know if he was right. Maybe he was. Maybe he wasn't. Time will tell.

About two years ago I was on a trip through Central Eastern Europe and I got into talking with a shop owner in Montenegro.

He said that he lived in Germany for 17 years. He spoke perfect German. He said he was from Hamburg. His family escaped the war in Yugoslavia in the nineties.

And then all of a sudden they had to leave Germany. After 17 years. I didn't even know that it was possible to be kicked out of a country just like that after having stayed there for 17 years.

And then he pointed at a big and very rundown building right across the street. It looked like it could house hundreds of families. He told me that half of the people living there won't have a thing to eat for dinner tonight. Looking at the building it seemed very likely.

And there I was, 28 years old, quit my well paid job not too long ago, had written and unsuccessfully published my first book and wasn't really sure what to do next.

And now this guy I just met told me that I did the biggest mistake ever. That quitting my safe job might have been the worst thing I could have done. That was quite a bit of a downer I have to admit.

Especially having been told this by someone like him who went through a lot of struggle in his life and is now living in quite a depressing city where many people can't even afford three meals a day. And in such a situation you can't just tell someone that you're trying to follow your dreams. That just doesn't work.

That was about two years ago.

And sometimes I have to think about him. But not about the lesson he wanted to teach me. No, but about the lesson he taught me without even noticing. Without knowing. Or maybe he knew exactly what he was doing. I don't know.

The real lesson he taught me was that you have to keep fighting. No matter the circumstances. No matter how hard it'll get. No matter what.

After all, he was a guy who lived his whole life in Germany, a rather wealthy country. And then all of a sudden he and his entire family were kicked out out of the country he grew up in and they had to go and live in a country he's never been to before. A country that was and still is suffering from what happened during the war. A country, heck an entire region that never really recovered from what happened.

This would probably have broken most people. I'm sure it would have broken me. Forever. I don't know if it broke him. I'm sure it was a horrible time for him. But there he was, standing right in front of me in his own shop and telling me that he has a family and kids.

I'm sure he's still struggling. More than I probably ever will. I'm sure it's not easy. And probably never will be easy for him. And I'm thankful that I never had to go through such an experience. And I hope that I will never have to go through a similar experience.

And to this day I'm still thankful for the lesson he (unknowingly) taught me two years ago. He was probably one of the greatest teachers I've had in my life so far. Because he taught me one simple thing...

If everybody around you stops running because it starts raining, then you've gotta keep running.

If everything around you seems to be falling apart, then you've gotta keep running.

If you feel like giving up, you've gotta keep running.

You've gotta run faster than you ever ran before...

The one & only reason I quit my job

I loved my job. I loved everything about it.

The free coffee. The lunch breaks. The subsidized food. Coming back home early. Random meetings in the middle of the day to have a cup of coffee. Living in Berlin. In New York. Having more money than I could possibly ever spend.

Heck, it was probably the best time of my entire life.

The greatest thing about having a job is that you're basically outsourcing responsibility for your whole life to someone else. All you have to do is to sign a piece of paper, agree on a monthly payment and then every single month things will be taken care of. The good life!

And after that? What did I have after I quit my job?

Well, here's what I got in exchange. For the next 3 years I was constantly trying to figure out where and how I'll be able to make enough money so that I won't be losing money every single day.

What about coming back home early? Gone!

What about the subsidized food? Gone!

What about the free coffee? Gone!

The coffee breaks? Gone!

Everything fun? Gone!

And what did I get in exchange?

In exchange every single day felt like I was getting robbed. It's like your life is a constant and never ending skydive. Adrenaline keeps pumping through your veins the whole time. It forces you to stay awake. All the time. It holds you back from sleeping. Even if you really want to, no have to go to sleep, you just can't.

And then the next morning when you wake up you feel even more tired than you felt the night before. But you just can't sleep anymore because of millions of things going through your head...

What the heck can I do to stop the ATM machine showing me less and less money every single time I check my balance? What will not work out today? How can I make my day longer than 24 hours? Will the thing I've worked on for the past two months work out? Will this be a good day? Ahhhh!

And then the adrenaline starts to kick back in...

Look. Many people don't realize it. But a job is probably the best thing that could ever happen to you. So if you have a job, try to keep it for as long as you possibly can. Enjoy it for as long as you can. Because it might be gone soon.

So why do I even do what I'm doing? Why didn't I just keep my job, get a paycheck at the end of each month and live the good life, without all the robbing and skydiving?

That's a really good question.

And here's what I usually tell people I meet that ask me this exact same question...

I feel that I have a lot more potential than this.

I feel that I'm underused.

I feel that I could use my life to do something bigger.

Something else. Maybe something bigger. I don't know.

I feel that I can change a thing or two. No matter how big or small.

What I realized working a corporate job for two years is that no one will ever be able to unleash my potential.

That no company in the entire world will ever be able tap into your strengths.

That no one is going to save you.

That no one is waiting for your genius.

That if you think you're special, then you'd have to prove it.

I'd have to prove it.

What I finally realized after having worked for almost two years is that the only person that's able to unleash my potential is me.

And no one else.

That the only person who's going to save me is me.

And no one else.

And that's the one and only reason why I really quit my job.

Because I realized that if I want to unleash my potential and figure myself out, then I'd have to do it myself. Because no one else ever will.

I realized that waiting for someone or something is useless.

Because no one will be able to help you. Ever. Only you can.

And this is the one thing that gets me up every single morning.

The one thing that keeps me going.

The one thing that keeps me up working late at night.

The one thing that helps me to get back up again every single time I've been knocked out.

This is the one thing that motivates me. The one and only thing thing that drives me.

I want to prove it to myself that I have it. That I have more than just this. Whatever that really means. Here's the thing...

I know that many people feel the same way. That they feel like they could achieve a lot more. That they have a lot more potential. But they're all just waiting. And then they get stuck. Because they're waiting for the signal to start their race.

But there's no signal. There never will be a signal. You have to give yourself that signal. You have to be the one who starts your race. Because no one else ever will. Only you can. And if you keep waiting for that signal you're only going to wait your entire life away. Without ever starting your real race.

So if you think you're special, if you feel like you could do better than this, if you feel that you have what it takes, if you feel that you have a lot more potential, then I challenge you to do so. To prove it.

And if you don't have the balls, if you don't feel like you could possibly do any of this, well then the simple truth is that you probably don't have it. That you probably aren't that special after all.

And if you don't believe in yourself, no one else ever will. It all starts with you. And no one else. If you don't trust in yourself and aren't confident enough that you're able to pull this off, then no one else ever will. Then no one else will ever trust in you. It all starts with you. And no one else.

If you're not going out there and aren't trying to figure out how to tap into your strengths then no one else ever will. It all starts with you. And no one else.

I know this is tough medicine. But I think it's something a lot of people out there have to hear. It's something I also had to hear myself a few years ago.

If you don't believe in yourself, then you might not be so special after all.

Then you might not have what you think you have.

And then you can go back to your job and live a happy life. Because you know that you don't have it.

Is that a bad thing? No, I think it's really liberating.

When you realize that you don't have it, that you're not so special after all, when you get out there and try to unleash your potential, do everything you possibly can and it just doesn't work out, then you'll realize that you maybe just don't have it. And when you realize that you don't have it then you'll be ready to settle.

Then you can stop watching all of these motivational videos. Then you can stop reading all of these blog posts. All of these books.

Because you'd know once and for all that what you're currently doing is the best you can do. The best for you. You don't have to buy into that self help crap anymore. You just know...

And to me, I'm going to say it again, that's fucking liberating. No more doubts. No more "what if". No more "can I do better than this?". It's all over when you try it and it just doesn't work out.

And that's why I fight so hard every single day.

I want to figure out whether or not I have it. Whether or not I might be able to tap into my strengths. Heck, whether or not I even have any potential at all. And that's what drives me. Every single day. It's an all in or nothing thing.

No one wants to admit that he or she just doesn't have it. It's brutal. And painful. But that's the only way to eliminate the voices in your head. The voices that are constantly telling you that you could do better than this. That you have what it takes.

And the moment you fail, the moment you realize it just didn't work out you can go back to cubicle nation. And live the good life. Because you know. You know that you just don't have it.

And this can be the most liberating thing in the world.

And to me, that's the single biggest problem of my generation. Heck, probably of all generations that have ever lived in a world or a country of abundance where you have the choice to do what you want to do. Where you're not forced to do things...

Most people are just too damn afraid to face the truth. It scares the shit out of them.

The fact that they might not be so special after all. That they might not have it scares the shit out of them. Out of you. Out of me. Out of everyone.

So we never really try.

And instead we keep waiting.

We keep waiting our lives away.

Please, don't be one of them.

Please, give yourself a chance to shine...

My life is falling apart

I didn't know what was going on. What to do. I had just quit my job. And now this. Why? How will I ever be able to get out of this mess?

2013 was the year where I lost myself. I quit my job to write a book. I had no clue about how to write a book. I had never written anything in my life before. No blog. No book. No nothing. As a matter of fact I was pretty bad at writing. Just ask my high school teacher Mr.. hmm I forgot his name.

It was a daily struggle. I was probably writing material for ten books. But nothing made any sense at all. Nothing fit together. It was mostly nonsense. So the doubts started to kick in. And they were eating me alive little by little. More and more every single day.

I tried everything I could and was working on it nonstop. But I couldn't piece it together. It was a total mess. I was a total mess. I was constantly stressed out. I was constantly in a bad mood. I wasn't getting enough sleep. Worrying about this. And then that.

Even worse, at my lowest my girlfriend broke up with me. I was living with her at her place after I came back from New York. I never owned any furniture. And never had a place of my own. So it didn't make sense to look for an apartment. So I moved in with her.

After all, I didn't even know where I'd be living next. Or what would happen next. I didn't know anything. Looking back at the whole thing, the conditions were just bad. Really bad. Probably for everybody involved. It was an apartment for two people. And back then there were basically four people living in that apartment. Non stop.

Her room mate just got engaged to a guy from Indonesia she met traveling. He was a tattoo artist. He wasn't allowed to work in Germany. And she was still studying. So they were basically at home 24/7. I tried to work at my old university's library.

It was rather quiet and a good spot to get some stuff done. They also had a cheap canteen with cheap food. I still had my canteen card from back in the days. So almost two years after I graduated I went back to where I came from. Just like they say in the song...

"From the bottom to the top." Just the other way round...

The funny thing is that when I studied there I never went to the library. I never ate at the canteen. I basically never went to my university at all. And now here I was. Eating cheap canteen food and sneaking into the university library every single day. Even on the weekends.

It was my choice. I wanted to write that damn book. And I didn't even know why. And that damn book cost me almost everything I had. Not only did it cost me 10 months of my life writing it and tens of thousands of dollars of income that I didn't get, but it also cost me my girlfriend from back in the days.

It was all my fault. It's always my fault. And if you think something is not your fault, then think again. I guarantee you that it will almost always be your fault. It's never your bosses fault. Or the economies fault. Or the stock markets fault. Argh, that damn stock market! You might only realize it later down the road, but trust me...

It's always your fault. Just like it's always my fault.

But that's ok. As long as you realize that it's always your fault. And no one else's. Because the moment you blame someone else you're outsourcing responsibility. And when you're outsourcing responsibility you're missing out on some of the biggest lessons life wants to teach you. So you'd better listen. And skip the blaming. And take all the blame instead.

So here I was. Working at my former university's library. Eating cheap canteen food. No place of my own. Not knowing what to do next. And all of this just after I quit my job and started writing my first book. I didn't have a lot going for me back then I have to admit.

So back in 2013 I had to move back in with my mom. I had to take my backpack full of stuff and once again go back to where I came from.

"From the bottom to the top." Just the other way round...

At that time I was 29 years old. I got myself into this mess. So I had to somehow get myself out of this mess again. I was the only one able to get myself out of this mess. I was the only one able to save me. And no one else.

Sure, I could have applied for another job. I just quit my job a few months ago. I could probably have found another job. But that's not what I wanted to do. I didn't want to give up after just a few months into this whole thing. I wanted to finish it. I wanted to see whether or not I could make it. Whether I would be able to tap into my strengths and unleash my potential. Whether I had the potential I thought I had.

If I failed at it, it would have meant that I might not be so special after all. It would have meant that I don't have more potential than I thought I had. That I didn't have it.

And that's something that I didn't want to accept. Not so early into the whole thing. It's been just a few months. That's why I kept fighting. That's why I'm still fighting today. Because I want(ed) to prove myself that I'm capable of this.

Of what?

Of all of this...

That's what pushes me every single morning. That's what keeps me working late. That's what keeps me pushing through the downs. I just don't want to give up and accept the fact that I might not be so special after all. That I don't have it. That's really all that got me going back then. And still does today.

I didn't want to and go back to cubicle nation and admit that I don't have it. Not now. I didn't want to give up before I haven't tried everything I could. Because I knew that I would regret it for the rest of my life if I didn't.

Look. Failure and giving up is ok. It's normal. It's human. Not getting it right is part of the process of getting it right. But only when you've done absolutely everything you can and it still doesn't work out should you give up.

Giving up without having tried everything you can is the worst thing ever. It's probably even worse than not starting at all. So I had to keep pushing.

I decided to keep pushing forward, to finish that book and see where it might take me. I decided to not apply for another job, even though pretty much everybody asked me when I would go back to do something with my life. People still ask me that today. But it got less over the years.

I didn't really have a clear plan about what I should or could do next. So I started reading books. I was never a big reader. Until the age of 28 I read maybe 10 books in total. But because I decided to write a book I bought a Kindle and started reading a lot of books. Because the only way to become a better writer is to read a lot. That's at least what I thought back then.

Now I know that the only thing that will make you a better writer is to write a lot.

Nonetheless, that's what I did back then. I read all sorts of books. Books on all sorts of different topics. Reading always helps when you're down on your knees. And I was down on my knees. And didn't know what I should do next.

I don't know how or why but I came across a book called *Love Your Like Your Life Depends On It* by Kamal Ravikant. I think it was suggested to me by Amazon because I bought *The Power Of Now* a while ago. And both of these books were pretty good. But I don't want to talk about these books right here.

I want to talk about something else here. I want to talk about an author I discovered through Kamal's book. In his book Kamal was talking about a guy I had never heard of before. His name was James Altucher.

And apparently that James guy was the guy who told Kamal to write and publish his book. He told Kamal that he never publishes anything on his blog if he's not embarrassed. If he's not afraid of what people might think of him.

And as I also started a blog back then, mainly to promote my upcoming book, I got curious. So I started reading all of his work. I bought all of his books. Read almost his entire blog. Read everything he posted on Facebook. On Twitter. Everywhere.

His writing gave me strength. He went through so much more than I could ever imagine. Everything I went through seemed like a piece of cake. He had made millions of dollars multiple times. And then lost all of it. Over and over again.

He lost his house, his marriage and everything went down the drain for him. He was suicidal. But he bounced back, every single time. And he's still alive today as I write this. Probably more so than he ever was before.

His books and articles gave me strength. The strength I needed to push through all of this. The strength and guidance I needed back then. Without him my life would probably be very different today. I think if it wasn't for his work I would probably have given up a long time already.

I would probably have returned to cubicle nation a long time ago. And you wouldn't be reading these lines right here.

And because I've learned so much from him, I decided to write down a few things I learned. The things that helped me the most when I was down on my knees. Maybe they'll also help some of you.

Here's what helped me to stop my life from falling apart back in 2013. Some of these things are from James and some of these things might be from someone else. Some of it might even come from me. I don't really remember. And it doesn't really matter.

So here's what got me where I am today...

reinvention

It's ok to start all over again every once in a while. As a matter of fact it's an absolute necessity to reinvent yourself and your life over and over again. Especially in the times we live in today where everything changes so fast that it's hard to even keep track of what's old and what's new. Reinvention is an absolute necessity and nothing to be ashamed of.

age

James Altucher is 47 years old or something like that. And he still reinvents himself every few months. He has started 20 or so businesses and 17 of them have failed. He wrote more books than I can remember. He went from employee to entrepreneur, from entrepreneur to hedge fund manager to venture capitalist and then back to being an entrepreneur. And now he does all of these things at the same time. It's never too late to try something new!

losing yourself

If you never lose yourself you'll never be able to truly find yourself.

saying no

To things other people suggest to you that you don't feel like doing. Saying no to the things that don't align with your overall vision.

saying yes

To the things and opportunities you created yourself. By constantly planting seeds that might some day in the future grow into a strong enough tree, into a big enough opportunity you can say yes to.

no one is going to save you

You have to stop to wait for others to chose you. Because no one will ever chose you. If you keep waiting for your boss, your friends or any other person to choose you, you'll be waiting your life away. You have to choose yourself, first and foremost. And then people will automatically start choosing you. No one is able to unleash your potential. Choose yourself.

writing

If you don't feel embarrassed by what you write, don't hit the publish button. Because if you're not embarrassed no one is going to read it.

being different

There are 7 billion people on this planet. And if you're doing what all the other 7 billion people are doing, you'll be competing with those 7 billion other people. So instead of doing what everybody else is doing, just be yourself and compete only with yourself.

failure

Not getting it right is part of the process of getting it right. Sure, some people get it right the very first time. But most of us just don't.

#diversification

Just having a job is the riskiest thing out there. Because if you lose your job, you'd lose your only stream of income. And that's what's really risky.

Betting on one thing and one thing only. So try to make sure you're always spreading your risk across multiple streams of income instead of believing that your job is safe. Because it isn't...

And that's how you go from the bottom to the top.

And not the other way round..

What I learned after writing 532 blog posts and 7 books

I still suck at writing...

My blog says that I wrote 532 blog posts. My Amazon page shows 7 different book titles. And I still suck at writing.

Even though I probably passed the magic 10,000 hours a long time ago I'm still far away from mastery. Not only this. I'm far away from being among the best of the best in my field.

Nonetheless, I feel like I've learned a thing or two about writing. And because most of the advice on writing out there is pretty repetitive, I'll try to focus on the things you've probably never read anywhere else, yet.

And yes, I'm not among the best in the field of writing, so I'm not qualified to give you any advice on writing. But whatever...

BS in. BS out.

If you constantly read listicles and useless garbage, then you'll also produce useless garbage. Try to be as selective as possible about what you read online. I read maybe 2-3 people online. And yes. This is a listicle...

Trust

People only read your stuff when they trust you. After all, reading an article is a commitment. It's an investment. It's a time investment. And time is one of the most important things we have. So don't buy into this storytelling BS out there that it's necessary to write 2000 words long posts. If I don't know you, if I don't trust you, if I don't believe that you're worth my time, then I'll just not read your stuff.

I know. Writing is art. But the best art in the world will not be looked at or appreciated when we don't know the person it's coming from. So make it easier for people to find out about you. To trust you. And to read your stuff. Shake it up every once in a while and don't just write stuff that's so long that no one is going to finish it. Don't believe all of this storytelling BS.

Reinvention

Try to shake things up every once in a while. Write short posts. Long posts. Post videos. Pictures. Reinvent yourself. Constantly. Do what nobody else is doing. Do what everybody else is afraid of. Do something that's against your "brand." That might hurt your "brand". Don't think about the consequences. Just think about shaking things up every once in a while to keep things fresh...

Brand

By the way, if you're constantly worried about your brand, you probably don't have a brand...

Have a day

If you don't have an exact day dedicated where you write and publish that blog post, it will never happen. Consistency is key. And for me, the best thing I ever did was to write and publish one post a day. Simply because it takes away every decision and time wasters of writing. When you write every day (or every Tuesday and Thursday or whatever), then you won't have to worry about what to write about, when to write, when to publish, will it be good enough and some more useless thoughts. All you've gotta do is write. And then hit the publish button. No matter what.

Write what you know

I know. This advice might seem simple. Still, most people don't seem to follow it. Most people write about things they have no clue about. They write about the stuff they have read somewhere else. And you know what happens when you write about something that you have no clue about? The first thing that's going to happen is that you'll sound like everybody else out there. And the second thing is writer's block. The only time I ever had writer's block in my life was when I tried to write about something I didn't really know that much about. Simply because if you haven't done it yet, if you have no clue about it, then you won't have enough stuff to write about...

Write about your thoughts

Write about the things you think about. Not only will this help you to kill writer's block, but it will also make your writing more authentic. Because you write down your thoughts. In your own voice. And that's authenticity. The stuff people like. But what if you only have crappy thoughts? See #1. BS in. BS out.

Talk to yourself

Everything I write, every piece of advice I give is advice I give to myself. So that maybe one day I might be able to follow my own advice and become a better person.

Don't start

If you're already super busy and your schedule just doesn't allow it, then please don't start writing. Or whatever it is thag you want to do. If you don't have the time to write, if you don't have the time to improve your writing, then you'll never be able to see any results. No one will heart your stuff. No one will like it. And because we're all humans with feelings and emotions this will only drag you down. No matter how much you say you're doing this just for yourself. Because at the end of the day you'll be frustrated if you don't get any feedback at all. That's just how we humans roll. And then when it gets you down all of the other stuff you're doing will also be affected. Like your job. Your relationships. And what not. So please, do yourself a favor and don't start publishing your stuff online if you already know that you don't have enough time..

Home runs

That being said, not every article you publish has to be a home run. As a matter of fact most of your articles will be just ok. Just like most of my articles are just ok. Just like most of Seth Godin's articles are just ok. I need to write maybe 20 blog posts to write one really good blog post. Maybe more. So how can you write more really good blog posts? I don't know about you. But for me, the second point works. Trust through writing more...

Talk less

Sometimes I don't talk to anyone for days. The more you talk, the less time you'll have to think. And the less time you'll have to think, well you know the results. You can see it every day on TV and in the news.

Read less

Reading doesn't make you a better writer. Only writing does make you a better writer. So stop reading your 5000th blog post about how to become a better writer and get going. Sit down and write. And then never ever stop again!

Be everywhere

People constantly ask me where they should write. "Should I start my own blog? Should I write on Medium? What about Quora? What's the best platform for me to get started?" Here's the thing. I don't know! Be everywhere. Publish your stuff everywhere. You've gotta be everywhere. You've gotta be where your readers are. And not where you want them to be.

I don't know

I use this all the time. Why? I don't know.

The first two

The first two lines and the last two lines are the most important ones. The first two lines because if they suck, people will stop reading. And the last two lines because if they're good, then people are going to hit the share or that like button...

Break the chain

You might think you can skip writing for a day. Or a week. No problem. But that's wrong! The moment you break the chain, you'll get sloppy. And the first time you skip it won't be the last time. You'll do it over and over and over again. Until it's been a few months since you wrote that last piece and then it's pretty much over. It's possible to skip writing for a few days. But it's so damn hard to get back into the flow. Not impossible. Just very, very hard.

Copy

No matter what you do, copy the hell out of someone who has already successfully done what you want to do. But always remember the first rule. Limit your consumption to a maximum of 5 people whose stuff you read. BS in. BS out.

No money

No one makes money writing anymore. Maybe the people who started blogging and writing 20 years ago still do. But everybody else just doesn't make enough money to survive, just by writing. Maybe the top 0,1% do. And the rest of us have to find other ways to be able to pay the bills.

But the most important rule of them all is that you should ignore all writing advice out there. Including this one. Especially this one...

How to succeed when you've failed at almost everything

I've failed at almost everything I did over the past 7 years...

I've started a clothing brand in China and it failed miserably. Then I've worked a corporate job for almost two years and quit it. After that I even started working for another company, but I quit that job after less than a month, too.

I've started more than 10 different websites. I've shut all of them down. I've written 7 books in the past 3 years (not including this one right here). And none of them was a bestseller. I've published 533 blog posts. And none of them went viral.

And I learned something very important over the past 7 years...

It's ok to fail. Everyone fails. Every once in a while.

It's ok to be frustrated and disappointed in yourself.

It's ok to not always reach your goals or the milestones you've set for yourself when you were young.

Because life is mostly about failure.

And success happens only every once in a while.

Not getting it right is part of the process of getting it right.

Look. Failure sucks. And it feels terrible. But sometimes we just can't avoid it. I know, it would be a lot better if we all succeeded at everything we do. But that's just not the reality for most of us. So we have to take it for what it is...

It's a process.

And that process leads from one thing to the next. Simply because no failure means that it's over. One failure doesn't mean that it's the end of the game. One lost match, one lost set doesn't mean you've lost the entire game.

Unless you decide that it's the end. Only if you decide to give up for good does it mean that it's the end. That you've failed for good.

But what failure really means is that you're just getting one step closer to getting it right. You're climbing up the ladder. One step at a time. And every step is part of the process. That process of getting it right.

Sure. Some people get it right the very first time. And it would be a lot nicer if we would all get everything right at the very first time. But most of us just don't. And when I say us, what I really mean is me.

So here's the thing...

If I didn't start that company back in 2009 in China, then I would never have gotten my next job, which got me into early stage investing for a bit.

And if I hadn't done that job, I wouldn't have written my first book. And if I hadn't written my first book, I would never have given 30+ talks at all sorts of conferences and events. And if I hadn't written my first book I wouldn't have written 6 more books. And I wouldn't have written more than 500 blog posts.

And then you wouldn't be reading the stuff you're reading right now.

And it's not about giving up when it gets hard. It's not about quitting when it gets tough. And it never was. In fact it's about trying everything you can when it doesn't work out. It's about tripling your efforts when it doesn't work out.

And then, once you've done everything you can, it's about moving on. It's about moving on and using the skills, the tools and the techniques you've learned and applying them to the next piece of your puzzle. So that you'll constantly be improving your process, yourself and your game.

And then it'll only be only a matter of time until you get it right.

How long will it take?

I don't know. If you think it's going to take 1 year, it'll probably take 10 years. If you think it'll take 2 years, then it'll probably take 5 years. And so on...

Is it worth it?

I don't know.

Is the unexamined life worth living?

You tell me...

The last safe investment

The stock market is lying to you. Self help books are lying to you. I am lying to you. The entire world is lying to you.

Everything you read about following your passion is complete BS. You won't be able to pay your bills following your passion only. That just doesn't work.

It'll take years and years until you might be able to pay your bills by following your passion. How do I know? I don't know. And I don't really know you. But I do know that in the whole year of 2015 when I was only following my passion and trying to make a living with it, I made less than other people pay rent for their apartments. A month.

So every blog, book, magazine or person telling you that you'll be able to follow your passion and make money doing so is basically lying to you. They are in the business of selling you dreams. I'm in the business of selling you dreams. I'm just really, really bad at it. That's how we make money.

We make money by telling you that all of this is possible. That you can live your dream. That you might one day be able to break free, live your dream, be happy, feed your family and buy a house. Look. Every second you spend reading this stuff people make money.

So stop reading this stuff! Stop reading my blog. My books. Everything. Go for a walk instead. Enjoy nature. Call your parents. Go for a run.

As a matter of fact, the more you buy into this stuff and the more time you spend on people's blogs or reading their books, the less likely it is that you're ever going to do things.

All of this stuff will pull you away from living the life you want to live. The life you should live. Could live. And instead you do nothing. You just keep reading.

And it puts more and more money in people's pockets. Into the pockets of the people that are trying to sell you dreams. That's their business model. That's my business model.

It only hurts you and your dreams. It takes away your time, energy and focus from the things that really matter. It takes away your focus from planting your seeds. And if you don't spend time planting seeds you will never be able to create your own freedom.

Instead you'll become a dreamer, an admirer, a passive participant of this entire dance. You become the gal watching everybody else dance. You're stuck watching other people planting their seeds. You watch them dance.

But you need to stop wasting your time and start dancing instead. Join the dance. Plant your seeds. Watch them grow. Fall in love. Break up. Fall into a deep hole. And then get back up again. Love this life. You only got this one life. So don't waste it!

But enough with this motivational jibber jabber. What does all of this even mean?

Here's what it means...

Keep your job for as long as you can. Don't ever quit your job. No matter how miserable it makes you feel. And at the same time try to save as much money as possible. Or build a business on the side and quit your job once it generates as much as you earn right now. It's up to you.

But why should you stay at a job that makes you feel miserable?

Because it's not your job that makes you feel miserable. It's not the people who make you feel miserable. Or your boss. What really makes you feel miserable is that you don't know why the hell you're even doing all of this.

Because you have no purpose in life. And that's really why your job drags you down. Why you hate your boss. Not because he's an asshole. He probably is. But because you have no clue why you're even doing all of this. And by the way, your boss probably thinks the same thing about you. Because he also doesn't have a purpose.

So why not try this instead?

Why not try to make it the purpose of your job to be able to save as much as possible. So you can one day invest in yourself. And buy yourself some freedom. To figure yourself out. And what you really want to do with your life. Life is expensive. So you can't just quit your job and try to figure yourself out with no money in the bank.

So why not work for two or three years and try to save as much as you can? Maybe even take a second job. And then, once you have enough money in the bank you can go ahead and quit your job. And invest in yourself. And buy yourself some freedom. And do all sorts of things you think you might enjoy doing.

Do things. Start things. Create things. Because only when you do things, when you create things will you be able to figure out who you are deep down inside. Why you are here. It only works this way.

And that's your purpose right there. That's your goal right there. That's your reason for getting up every single morning. To save as much as you can so you'd be able to buy yourself some freedom and invest in yourself.

Look. I'm not saying that you should save on Starbucks coffee or stuff like that. Or that you should do this for the rest of your life. No. That would be total nonsense. Just do it for a while and avoid buying big and unnecessary stuff you know you don't need.

And to me, that's a pretty good purpose right there. Even if it's just temporary. Maybe it works for you. Maybe it doesn't. It worked for me. I always knew that I'm only doing my job to be able to save enough money to be able to figure myself out.

And this is what got me up every single morning. That's what kept me going. What kept me pushing. It was my fuel. That's how I found a temporary purpose in what I was doing and I actually started enjoying it. A lot.

Because I knew that without that job I would never be able to go to the next level. That I would never be able to buy myself some freedom without that job. Because starting a business on the side just didn't work out for me. So I was thankful that I had that job.

Without that job that allowed me to save enough money I would never have been able to invest in myself and buy myself some freedom.

Without that job that helped me to buy myself some freedom you wouldn't be reading these lines right here...

What's your worst case scenario?

My worst case scenario happened to me more than once over the past 7 years. And I'm not talking about the worst case scenario where the entire world collapses. No, I'm talking about a realistic worst case scenario.

The worst case scenario in my head was that I would end up living on the streets somewhere in El Salvador. Sorry, if you're reading this and are from El Salvador. I'm sure it's a nice country. It's just such a small country that I thought no one from there would read it.

Funny enough, when I published this part on Medium someone from El Salvador asked me why I think it was such a bad country. My bad. So I apologize in advance already.

But now back to the story. My realistic worst case scenario was that I had to move back in with my mom.

And I had to move back in with my mom multiple times over the past 7 years. As a matter of fact, whenever I'm in my hometown in Munich, I stay at her house. Because I don't have a place of my own. Nowhere.

Now if you say, oh well, that's not really such a bad worst case scenario, then think about it for a second. Take a second and think about your realistic worst case scenario.

What's your worst case scenario?

Chances are that your worst case scenario is quite similar to mine. The only difference might be the country you're living in. We all have family. Or friends, don't we?

And if you don't get along with your parents anymore, then make sure you figure your shit out before they die. Or you might regret it for the rest of your life. Same goes for friends.

If the shit hits the fan and the things you've worked on didn't work out as you hoped they would, then it's very likely that your worst case scenario is similar to mine and not that bad after all.

Am I privileged? Yes, I am. I am privileged to have family and friends.

And the truth is that the horror scenarios we have in our heads, the ones where we're going to end up broke on the streets of New York City or in the slums of Rio de Janeiro never really come true. It's just our minds playing tricks on us.

So take a minute and think about it, for real.

What's your worst case scenario?

Even if it does look different from mine and instead you'd have to move in with one of your friends, your boyfriend or girlfriend, or move into a smaller apartment, these things aren't usually that bad after all.

For me, moving in with my mom gave me the chance to get to know her a lot better. Today, I appreciate the time I'm able to spend with my mom or my dad a lot more than I did a few years ago.

After all, our time here on this planet is limited. And you never know. It could be over tomorrow.

And having had to move back in with my mom and really getting to know her as a person and not just as my mom might have been one of the best things that happened to me over the past couple of years.

Simply because I won't have any regrets. And she won't either. I won't have any regrets that I didn't spend enough time with her. That I didn't ask the things I always wanted to ask. That I didn't say the things I always wanted to say.

Sure, I was sort of "forced" into this situation. Sometimes you have to force yourself into do these kinds of things. I might probably not have done it if I didn't have to. Because I might have been too afraid of what other people might think of me.

And you know what?

Screw other people!

Be honest with yourself and spend a few minutes thinking about your worst case scenario. Think about what's realistically going to happen when the the shit hits the fan. When your world sort of falls apart.

And then, try to look at the bright side of it. Try to find the bright side. There's always a bright side. You just have to look long and close enough.

Sure, you might have to move into a smaller apartment. And your wife and kids might not enjoy it that much. But after all, maybe that's a good thing. Maybe that's a lesson in frugality for your kids. If I look around most kids today grow up way too spoiled.

But what do I know? I don't know what I'm talking about here. I have no kids. And no family. So I can't really say anything about it. All I know is that I learned frugality from my mom, who came as a refugee to Germany after Word War II with her family. They didn't have a thing when they came here. And that's how I was raised.

Look. You might temporarily lose a game or two, but at the same time there will always be a (small or big) win hiding somewhere.

As long as you're able to open your eyes again, to wipe your tears away and to look into the sun to see the bright side of life again...

Don't be an entrepreneur

Being an entrepreneur sucks.

It might be the worst decision in your life to become an entrepreneur.

Especially if what you're really looking for is freedom. Because entrepreneurship is a prison in disguise. And no one ever really talks about it. But it's really a prison.

No matter what type of entrepreneur you are. Being an entrepreneur is not about freedom. Simply because when you do your own thing, when you are out there on your own, no one really needs you. And when no one really needs you, when no one really cares about you, well then no one is going to end up buying your products. Or your services. Or whatever.

And when that happens, when no one ends up buying from you, when you don't get money at the end of each month, then you won't be able to pay for rent. Or food.

So if you think entrepreneurship is about freedom, think again. Because it really isn't. At least not in the first 5, 10 or even more years.

You'll always depend on someone else. You'll depend on your customers. On your partners. Or your investors. And all of these people are a lot harder to satisfy than your boss. Your boss won't fire you that easily. Unless you do something really, really stupid.

Simply because your boss works for his boss who works for her boss who works for her boss and so on. And at the end of the day no one really cares where all the money goes to. Or where it comes from.

When you work for a company, no one really cares about someone getting a salary 10 levels below them. No one even knows where all that money really comes from. Or where it ends up. But most importantly your boss is not paying you his own money. It's the company's money. That comes from somewhere. From where? No one really knows anymore. There are just way too many layers. So your boss couldn't care less.

Also, when you have a job, the biggest challenge is about getting hired. When you're hired you're pretty much set. Unless your company gets in trouble. Or they find someone who'll do your job for a lot less. Or they invent an algorithm to replace you. Then it's pretty much over.

On the other hand, when you're an entrepreneur the money comes straight from your customers. Or investors. And they care about their money. A lot. A lot more than your boss does. Because it's usually their own hard earned money.

Sure, being an entrepreneur is great. And I love it. And it's better than you might have imagined in your wildest dreams. It's probably one of the coolest things in the world.

But what entrepreneurship is not about, is freedom.

At least not in the first 5, 10 or maybe even 20 years.

I had to learn this the hard way.

Instead of working for the man, you'd be working for your customers. Or your investors. Or your partners. Or whatever. You'll be their bitch.

So you'll never really be working just for yourself. You'll always be working for someone else. You'll never be really free.

And this can in some cases turn into a prison. A prison called freedom...

On never giving up

I've given up many times. Too many times. More than I'd like to admit.

It's hard to keep pushing. Too hard sometimes. Sometimes you just want to give up. And then you just give up. And that's ok.

But all of the things I gave up so far had one thing in common.

They were all about chasing opportunities. That one cool idea I had. That one opportunity I saw.

But the thing about chasing opportunities is that they are just that. They are just opportunities.

They are not who you are deep down inside. They are not what you really want to do. They are now what you know you should be doing deep down inside. They're just a tool that might maybe help you to get to where you really want to be. A tool to help you do that one thing you always wanted to do.

It's always the same thing. We do all of these things so that we might maybe one day be able to do that one thing we have been dreaming about doing for a long, long time.

"I just need to finish this and then I can finally start doing what I really want to do in life. I just need to make enough money so I'm free enough to be able to do what I really want to do. I just need..."

But the truth is that you'll never finish this. Or that. You'll never have enough money. You'll never have enough of anything. You'll never be free enough.

The only way you'll ever be free is when you do the things you know you should be doing deep down inside of you. These are the things you should be doing. Instead of chasing opportunities. Because opportunities come and go. And you'll easily give up when the shit hits the fan.

But when you do the things you know you should be doing deep down inside, then you won't give up so easily. Then you'll keep pushing. No matter what. And if it doesn't work out, then you'll iterate. Then you'll try to find other ways to make it work. Until it does.

Because it's the only thing you can do. The only thing you know you should do. So you'll never give up. And you'll always find ways to make it work. To do it. No matter if it pays the bills or not. No matter if it's just a side project. It's all about doing it.

And that's why it's so important to start doing the things you know you should be doing right now. But don't rush it. Go one step at a time.

Doing these things will help you to keep pushing. These are things things that will help you to get you up every single morning. These are the things that will help you to become the best version of yourself. To be and find yourself. These are the things.

And nothing else...

The passive income lie (or how to build your personal brand)

There's no passive income...

Over the past 3 years I've launched more than 10 websites. I've written more than seven books. This one right here is my eights book. I've uploaded and designed dozens of t-shirt designs to platforms where people can buy them. I've written five or six guidebooks.

And none of these things generates passive income for me.

All of this passive income stuff is basically a lie. There's no way you can create a product, a service or what not and then leave it as it is. That never works. You'd always have to create new stuff to be relevant. To stay relevant.

But even more importantly, you've gotta become relevant first. You've gotta build an audience first. No matter what you're trying to sell or trying to make passive income with. If you don't have an audience you won't be able to make anything. So if you want freedom, travel the world and generate money online you've gotta build your audience first.

I've spent the last three years building my audience. And I worked a lot more on building that audience than I'd have spent time at a day job. And I'm still not able to generate passive income. Most of it is semi passive. Because you've gotta be active. You've gotta be out there. You've gotta put stuff out there. Because if you don't, people will forget about you. Instantly!

I once did a test and didn't post anything for an entire month. No one even noticed...

So the moment you stop showing up is basically the moment people forget about you. It's like you never even existed. No matter how important or unimportant the thing you're doing really is. You'll be replaced in no time by someone or something else. No questions asked.

There's no such thing as passive income. Or living on an island. And traveling the world while you see the cash rolling in. There's just hard work and constantly showing up. More often than anybody else.

For how long? I don't know. Maybe 5 years. Maybe 10 years. Maybe forever. But I really hope it's just 5 years.

Look. Most people who are selling you the passive income dream are basically showing you how to make passive income by teaching you the exact same technique they use. To teach other people how to make passive income. It's basically a big fat ponzi scheme where everybody makes money teaching everybody else how to make money online by teaching others again. There's no real value created. Just a big fat teaching scheme.

The only way to build an audience and to maybe one day make money online, to live in freedom and wherever you want to and do what you want to is to build your brand as they say.

Look. The people who are generating passive income are people who have a brand. Who stand for something. People like James Altucher. Or Gary Vaynerchuk. Tim Ferriss. Or Seth Godin.

None of them used any techniques or tricks to build their brands. They put in the work. For many many years. Because there are no other tricks that work other than putting in the work.

But even those folks don't really generate passive income. Because they've spent years and years and years building their brands. They invested more time than most people are willing to. And they still show up to this day.

Everybody can do what they are doing. But trust me, most people just won't.

So how do you build your brand?

I don't know how you can build your brand. I don't know you. I could tell you to do this or to do that. But the truth is that I just don't know. No one knows. Because it's different for everybody. But I guess being yourself and doing something unique instead of doing something that everybody else is already doing is a pretty good start.

I know this is hard. Because it's a lot easier to just do what everybody else is already doing. Because there's a roadmap out there for that. But guess what. That roadmap only works once. For the person who created that roadmap. But it won't work anymore for you. Because you're different. You are you. And no one else.

Look. I really can't tell you how to do all of this. But I can tell you how I did it. How I got where I am right now. Wherever that might be...

Back in 2013 I started writing a book. I wasn't ready for it. At all. I had no clue about how to write a book. And I was a bad writer. But I did it nonetheless. Why? Because I felt that there has to be more than my 9 to 5 job. Because I realized that no one would come and unleash my potential. That I was the only one able to unleash my potential.

At the same time when I started writing my book I started a blog. Actually, I didn't even start with a blog. I didn't know how to setup a blog. It was too technical for me back then. I wasn't ready. But I just did it. So instead of starting a blog I posted my updates on Facebook. And only a few months after I posted my first update on Facebook did I start my own blog.

Then when my book was half way done I went on a speaking tour. I wasn't ready. And I was scared. But I knew that I had to do it. That this was part of trying to unleash my potential. Because no one else ever would. I was scared because in the past people were making fun of me when I gave talks in public. And because no one knew me back then, I contacted 30 universities in Germany and asked them if they were interested in me giving a talk. I ended up giving ten talks or so.

And then I did the same thing again all over Europe and gave 15 or so more talks at all sorts of events and conferences. And because no one knew me back then, I got in touch with more than 30 people. And when I started that tour I had just one date confirmed. I wasn't ready. But I did it nonetheless and started that tour. And the rest is history as they say...

When the tour was over I decided to write another book. I still didn't feel ready. Especially because my first book wasn't a success. And right after I published it I was ashamed of it. And the only way to get rid of that shame was to write another book. A better book. And then another one. And then another one. Until maybe one day I won't be ashamed anymore of the books I write.

So I kept pushing. I kept writing books. I kept writing blog posts. I kept giving talks. And I still build new websites at least once every few months and experiment with new models and ways of doing things.

Look. When I started I didn't know anything about anything I'm doing right now. I didn't learn any of this at school. No one taught me any of this. And when I started, I was pretty bad at all of these things. But that didn't really matter. What matters is that you keep going and then keep improving.

And when you start at zero there's a hell lot of stuff you can improve. And the only way to learn this stuff is by doing. By getting out there. By standing in front of a crowd naked. By getting laughed at your face. That's the only way. There's no other way.

So bottom line is this...

You've gotta start when you're not ready. When you don't know who you are. When you don't know what exactly it is you want to do with your life. Because only by doing things, by experimenting, by tweaking over and over again will you be able to figure yourself out. Will you be able to find yourself.

And that's how you build your brand. And your audience. And maybe some years down the road you might even be able to become a free person and make money online. Maybe. Maybe not. But probably not...

It's all about sacrifice

And nothing else...

No matter what you're seeing, it's most likely not the reality. Because what you're seeing, what most people want you to see is the good stuff. They don't want you to see the bad stuff.

The stuff when they're down on their knees. When they are at the bottom. People only want you to see and show you the stuff when they're at the top. When everything goes well. They don't show you the stuff when they're at their lowest. At their worst.

So whatever you see online, read online or whenever someone tells you how awesome it is what he or she's doing, know that this is probably only true for 1% of the time. People don't talk about the other 99% of the time. They don't talk about the struggle. About the struggle they had to go through. And still have to go through today.

Because it might make them and their life choices look stupid. They only want you to see the good stuff. They want to hear you tell them that they're living the dream. That they've done everything right.

They don't want to look stupid in front of everybody else. I don't want to look stupid in font of everybody else. She wants you to think that she's living the life. When she clearly isn't.

Look. The truth is that all of this is about sacrifice. It's not about living on a dream island. It's not about living the life. It's not about freedom. It's all about sacrifice. And nothing else. The more you're willing to give up today, the more likely you're MAYBE going to get more in return some time in the future.

And I say maybe, because there's no guarantee for anything in life. You might be sacrificing things your whole life and you might never ever get anything in return. That's just the reality. And sometimes all the hustling in the world won't help. Sometimes it just doesn't work out. Ever.

And that's why it's so lonely at the top, as they say. Because most people are not willing to sacrifice anything. They're not willing to do things. All they're willing to do is to share stuff on their Facebook walls telling you the 7 habits of successful people. And that's already about it.

But what it's really all about is staying at home on Friday night when everybody else goes out drinking. It's about not seeing your friends as much as you'd like to. It's about staying in front of your laptop until your eyes turn red. Until you can't barely see anymore. Until they bleed. Ok, that's maybe a bit exaggerated. Or maybe it isn't. What do I know?

That's what it's all about. It's about sacrifice. It's about believing in yourself. And giving yourself a chance to shine. But you can only shine brighter than everybody else if you have enough fuel. And the fuel doesn't come from sitting around and waiting. It doesn't come from posting "hustle" on your Facebook wall.

It only comes from doing. From building momentum. And not from sitting around when you haven't achieved anything yet. I haven't achieved anything yet. That's why I've gotta keep pushing.

It's all about putting in more work than anybody else out there ever would for a few years. It's just like they say, you've gotta be willing to live a few years like no one else ever would, to be able to live the rest of your life like no one else ever could.

Whatever that might mean in your case.

And the reality is that everybody can do that. But no one ever does. That's also the reason why you'll most probably never get what you really deserve. What you really want.

Look. I left everything behind. I left my friends behind. I left my family behind. I don't own a thing anymore. No one hands me me a paycheck at the end of the month. I'm not working for anybody. And all I have with me right now is a backpack with a few things. The most valuable thing I have with me is my $300 laptop on which I'm writing this right here.

And many days are a struggle. Things that other people take for granted can turn into a struggle. And most of the time most of the things I do don't work out. And you only see the things that did work out. You never see the stuff that didn't work out. You never see the struggle.

Because I don't want to look stupid. Mostly because I sometimes really feel stupid. And think that I'm stupid. But you never get to see that. You only get to see the things where I look smart. And not stupid.

So the next time you see someone and think that they're living the life, then think again. They're probably not living the life. It's all about sacrifice. Until maybe one day it all pays off. Maybe it doesn't. Who knows? No one really knows...

And if those people are really living the life right now, then think about what they had to go through to live the life they're now living. Think about all the pain. Think about all the hardship. Think about all the struggle. And the sacrifice.

But most importantly think about this. And ask yourself this simple question...

Am I willing to go through all of this without any guarantee that it will ever work out?

Under these conditions, am I willing to give myself a chance to shine or just leave it as it is?

And then act accordingly.

And never ever look back again...

What are your three things?

You just need three things in life to be happy.

Nothing more. Nothing less. Just three things.

Not four. Not five or maybe even twenty. Just three things.

And whenever something doesn't fit into one of these three categories you have to get rid of it. Or don't do it. It will only distract you from what's really important in your life.

And when I say you, I basically mean me. And when I say three I mean it could be any other number that's manageable. But I think three is a good number.

So here are the three things that are most important in my life...

1. Freedom to do and live wherever I want to

2. Eliminate everything that causes unhappiness

3. Make my life as smooth as possible

And whenever I have to decide whether or not I should do something, I take a look at that list. And then I act accordingly.

Look. I get it. Not everybody can do that. Not everybody can act accordingly right away. I wasn't able to do that just a few years ago either. When I decided that those are my priorities I was far, far away from all of these three things.

And it took me many years of hard work and sacrifice to get to the point where I enjoy some of the above freedom. I'm still not quite there yet. But I'm getting there.

It's hard. Really hard. It's a daily struggle. There are forces that are constantly trying to pull you away from these things. From your things. From the things that are most important in your life. Whatever that might be.

Over the years many people asked me if I wanted to work with them. Or for them. They basically offered me the one thing I needed the most. They offered me money at the end of each month. But it was in exchange for my freedom.

And it was a tough call every single time. Because I didn't have that much money. Even worse, it got less and less every single day. I was losing money for 3 years every single day.

So rejecting these offers wasn't easy. At all. But all I wanted were those three things in my life. Those were and still are the three most important things for me. Right now. The only things that matter.

So I said "no" every single time I got offered a job or was offered to work with someone on a project. Simply because I knew that it would cost me some of my freedom. The freedom I fought hard for many years.

Look. I'm not going to lie to you. The only thing that helped me to get to where I am right now was that I went back to these three core principles over and over again and made these the basis for all of my decisions. And nothing else. Even, no especially when it was a tough call.

If I didn't do this, I would probably be stranded somewhere in the consulting jungle where I would always have to trade my time for money. And when you're trading your time for money, then you'll never be free. Ever.

Simply because you'll never be able to make enough money to enjoy more freedom. If you want to make more money, so you could afford more freedom, then you'd have to work more hours. Which means less freedom after all. So that doesn't really work.

I'm not saying that any of this is or was easy. It's probably the hardest thing out there to say "no" to making more money. It always looks like more money will mean more freedom. When the truth is that it doesn't.

It usually just means more work, less time and less freedom when you're working for someone. When you're trading time for money.

Look. When your family is the most important thing in your life, when your family is on that list, then that promotion might not be the best idea ever. Because every promotion means that you've gotta work more. Which basically means less time for your family.

You'd always have to keep trading time for money. So instead of trading more and more of your time for more money, try to start trading less of your time for money and use the additional time to build or create something that will help you to create your own freedom. Instead of destroying it.

So how do you get there? How do you create something that helps you to create your own freedom?

I don't know. I don't know you. I don't have all the answers.

But I think a good start is to stop trading more and more of your time for more and more money. Because this won't get you anywhere in the long run. Other than maybe the hospital.

And making your list with your three things of course.

It all starts with this.

It all starts with giving yourself some time to breathe.

Some time to think.

Some time to experiment.

Ultimately, it all starts with doing and creating things.

And nothing else...

You don't have to be rich to do what you want to do

You absolutely have to do what you want to do. Right now...

No matter how much or how little money you have or make. You have to do what you enjoy doing. Right now.

Because that's the only way you'll ever be satisfied. That's the only way you'll ever be happy. That's the only way you'll ever be able get what you deserve. Be it success. Money. Or whatever it is that you want.

If you constantly do things you don't enjoy doing your energy levels will run low. Maybe even too low. Until your batteries can't be recharged. Ever again.

Look. Only when you do the things you want to do and really enjoy doing will you be able to push through the tough times. Will you have enough energy to get back up again.

Only when you do the things you enjoy doing will you be able to be among the best of the best in your field.

Only when you do the things you really enjoy doing will work stop to feel like work.

A lot of people ask me how I'm able to do so much stuff. How I'm able to write so consistently. How I'm able to work on so many different things in parallel.

The simple truth is that I try to do as much of the things I enjoy doing. And I can do these things up to 16 hours a day without feeling tired. Without feeling annoyed. Simply because I enjoy doing these things.

Sure, 98% of the things I do right now are things that enable me to do that one thing I really enjoy doing.

I do a hell lot of stuff on the side to support my writing. Because I can't make a living writing. But I'm totally fine with it, because all of the things I do on the side to pay the bills are somehow related to writing and help me to keep writing.

And I'm not saying that you should quit your job and only do the things you enjoy doing. That's total nonsense. Like I said earlier, don't quit your job. Do it on the side. Save as much money as possible.

And in case that one thing of yours, that one thing you enjoy doing might maybe one day generate some cash so you can pay your bills, then feel free to take the leap and quit your job. Or don't. It's up to you.

But the thing is that you can do whatever you want to be doing without being rich. Right now.

I'm not rich. All I did was to follow my own advice. Well, actually, I didn't really follow my own advice. I only came up with this stuff once I've done all of this. Once I've saved enough money to be able to quit my job.

I also tried the side hustle thing which didn't really work out for me. Maybe it will work out for you. I don't know. But what I do know is that it took a hell lot of time. And that it didn't work from one day to the next. It took a few years. But you've gotta start. And then never ever stop again. No matter what.

And the most important thing right here and right now is that you start to realize that you don't have to wait until you're rich, until you have enough to do whatever it is that you want to do. Or say what you want to say. Or to be more honest.

You can do whatever you enjoy doing right now and right here.

If you think that you'll need enough f*ck you money, then no money in the world will ever be enough for you to do or say what you want to say.

Here's the truth...

You'll never have or make enough f*ck you money if you keep doing things you don't enjoy doing. Simply because doing things you don't really enjoy doing and working with people you don't really enjoy working with will always drain your energy.

And without that energy, you'll never be able to make it to the top. You'll never make it to your top. You'll never become the best version of yourself. And that's why waiting until you have enough will never work.

Only doing the things you enjoy doing will work. One step at a time. As a matter of fact, only doing the things you enjoy doing will help you to make enough.

Enough of what?

Enough of what it is that you want to make or have...

Your moment will come

But you've gotta be ready...

It doesn't happen overnight. Nothing happens overnight. And when it does happen, you've gotta be ready.

You've gotta be ready when that big wave hits. You've gotta be prepared to ride that wave, your wave, for as long as you can.

Look. Maybe your wave will come. Maybe it won't. No one really knows. But whenever it comes you should know how to catch that wave and ride it for as long as you can.

If that wave comes and you're not ready, if you don't know how to surf, then you might not be able to ride that wave. Maybe if you're a natural you'd be able to ride it for a few seconds. But that's already about it.

Alright. Enough waves for now. What does all of this even mean?

It means that you have to work on the foundation first. If people find out about you, you've gotta have a backlog of work already. So if that one big hit comes you'll be able to leverage it for the rest of your life.

Just the other day someone asked me if it's better to build an audience first and then release that killer article, book, product or whatever or to create that killer thing first and then build an audience on top of that.

And I think both ways won't get you anywhere. No one really knows what's going to be a killer product, article, book or whatever. All you can do is guess. And in 99.9% of the time that guess is wrong.

Whenever I though that an article would take off, no one even noticed. And whenever I thought that this post is the worst thing I ever wrote it took off. One of the most popular articles I ever wrote was called 5 minutes. It took me 5 minutes to write it. And it got more than 1,500 recommends on Medium.

Look. No one is able to predict the future. Or the market. Or the customers. Or anything. It just doesn't work.

All you can do is to put in the work, be patient, consistent, create opportunities for yourself and the people around you over and over again and get ready for your one big moment. That might or might not come.

You've gotta learn how to surf to be able to ride the big waves. Even the small ones...

Even if you might have a great idea for a product or what not, if you don't know how to properly execute it, if you've never executed anything before, then this big idea of yours will just remain that. A nice idea. That will never spread.

It's the same for everything in life. You've gotta put in the work first so that you'll be ready when that one big moment comes. People say it's about luck. It isn't. It's about being ready when that wave comes.

If you've never been on a date before, if you've never approached a man or a woman on the streets or in a bar, then you might never be able to do so when you meet the man or the woman of your dreams. You've gotta get ready.

Otherwise you might miss that one big shot you have. So you'd better get ready. And who knows. While getting ready that small shot might turn into your big shot.

But there's no guarantee. There's no guarantee for anything in life.

There's just trying and knowing.

Or not trying and never knowing.

It's your call...

Who's in your team?

Don't let them fool you...

I'm astonished by how many people tend to read or listen to advice online. I'm even astonished that so many people read my stuff.

And to me that's one of the biggest problems of my generation. Maybe even every other generation out there. There are so many gurus out there. And everybody says something else.

Someone might say this and then the other person might say that. So at the end of the day you're even more confused than you've ever been before. That's why the self help industry is so big. Because they're basically creating their own clients.

And because you might be even more confused than before, you'll always be looking for more and more answers and you'll end up consuming more and more stuff.

We've basically unlearned to find our own answers.

I get it. Sometimes you need advice. But not all the time. Just sometimes.

And what happens when you're always looking for answers elsewhere is that you'll never ever take action. Even though most of the stuff out there is about taking action and hustling, it does quite the opposite. It's just too overwhelming. Too much.

But the answers have and always will be inside of you. And nowhere else.

That's why it's called self help. And not someone else help.

Sometimes I even believe that we would be better off with most of this stuff. With less people like me. So we'd learn how to find our own answers again.

What you shouldn't forget when you consume all of this stuff online (just like this thing right here) is that most people make money saying this or saying that. Or that they plan on making money some time in the future. That's why there are so many out there. Because it's a business. It's a billion dollar industry.

But I think that's totally fine, as long as you're always aware out it. Always...

What I think is most important these days with the never ending supply of gurus and self help BS out there is to be able to navigate that jungle.

And what I found out to be working best for me over the years is to pick my top 3-5 people and then only consume their stuff.

Otherwise you might end up even more confused than you ever were before. And then you might never take action. And never get going.

I don't know if this works for you. But that's what I do. That's what works for me.

I only consume stuff online from 4 people. And nothing else from no one else. I've never read an article on Medium from someone else other than them. I don't read other people's blogs. I've never watched a video from someone else other than them. Ok, a few TED talks maybe.

I think that this is the new version of the "You are the average of the five people you spend most time with."

Sure, you can still consume other people's stuff. But try to spend as much time as possible with your "virtual team" or your real team in case they want to hang out with you.

If you spend too much time with too many different people at the same time you'll only end up being a superficial mix of too many different things.

You'll end up being a big mix of superficial and conflicting stuff when you read too many different things online from too many different people conflicting each other. But most importantly, you'll lose time reading. Time you could otherwise have spend doing.

So go out there and find your five people. Find the five people that inspire you. And don't just choose them because they are rich. Or successful. Or whatever external measure.

Choose them because they are the kind of person you want to be. Choose them because of their characteristics. And not because of what they have achieved. Most of the uber successful people don't seem to be so nice in real life after all.

Choose them because they've taken a similar path to yours. Choose them because they've taken a path you want to take.

And it doesn't matter what field they're coming from. They can come from every field and every discipline out there. It doesn't matter.

And it's not about copying them. Or being someone you're not. It's the exact opposite. It's about being yourself and finding out how you can make it work to be yourself.

It's about figuring out how they made it work for themselves. How they were able to get to where they are right now. It's about studying their past. Their history. Their strategies. And their techniques.

And then applying what you've learned to your own life. To being yourself.

To be able to get going, to move forward, to become the best version of yourself and to be able to unleash your potential.

You've gotta pick your team. You've gotta pick the five people you hang out with the most.

Why?

Because you are the average of the five people you spend most time with.

But then again, it's probably better if you find your own ways.

This is just my way.

This is just the way that works for me...

The thing you don't know about yet

It's never too late to start...

You can never be too old. Or too young. Or too busy.

The only thing that matters is that you start whatever it is that you want to start. And then you've gotta be patient. And consistent. And never give up. And be willing to get back up again over and over again.

And it's not about bumping your head against the wall over and over again doing the exact same thing. Sometimes it's about adjusting and implementing the things you've learned. And sometimes that means to move on and to do something else. To stop what you're doing right now. Even if it's just for a short while.

If no one reads your stuff after a few months of writing consistently good stuff then it"s about figuring out why no one even notices. Then it's maybe about figuring out how to build your audience online first. Authenticity and telling the truth won't get you anywhere if you don't have an audience.

Writing and they will come doesn't work. Just like build it and they will come doesn't work. Or create it and they will come doesn't work.

If no one listens to your podcast, buys your books, your products or what not then it might be a good time to figure out why no one is buying or listening. Maybe the demand is just not there. Maybe you've gotta learn how to build up the demand first. Maybe you've gotta learn how to sell.

There are many maybes. Hundreds. Heck, thousands. And you've gotta figure out your maybes. Otherwise you might never be able to keep doing what you're doing right now.

If the numbers on your bank account get smaller and smaller maybe it's time to go and work for someone else for a while and earn some cash so you can sleep again at night.

Look. Over the past 7 years I've done a lot of different things. And none of these things ever really worked out. But every little thing I did lead to the next thing. And then the next thing. Until this thing right here happened.

While I was still studying I started and failed at building a company. At the same time I was also teaching English. Then I went back to Germany and started working for a big corporation for about two years. Then I quit my job to write a book.

And that book lead to a speaking tour I organized myself across Germany. I sent dozens of emails to people who didn't know me and who I didn't know. And this again lead to a self organized tour through Central Eastern Europe. And a total of 7 more books. This one right here is the eighth.

I was trying to figure out how to build an audience. How to build up demand for what I was doing. Because I've learned the hard way over and over again that create it and they will come just doesn't work. No matter how good your product or service is. I've had to learn the basics. And then master them.

As I mentioned earlier already, I've also started 10 or so different websites. Some of them were making some money. Some of them didn't. I stopped working on all of them. But I learned how to create websites. How to send traffic to a completely new website. How to build an audience from scratch. I learned a bit of copywriting. And many more things.

And that's what it's really all about. It's about figuring out what works and what doesn't. It's about figuring out how you can achieve your three things. And once you're there, once you're able to live your life according to your three things you can move on to the next thing.

What next thing?

Well, the thing that comes next.

The thing that you'll do next.

The thing you don't know about yet.

The thing I don't know about yet.

And that's the beauty of it all.

There will always be something next.

Something more exciting.

As long as you allow that something next to happen…

This might be the most controversial part of this book

And a lot of you might not agree with me, but...

Everybody can do what I'm doing. Everybody!

And it doesn't matter how old or how young you are. Or how much or how little money you have. Or what your current job is. Or how big or small your mortgage is. Or in which country you live. Everybody can do it!

The only thing you need is a laptop and an internet connection. Heck, you can even do this with a smartphone. And I've been to some of the poorest countries in the world. And everybody has a smartphone there. And I don't even have a smartphone.

Just a laptop. A laptop is much cheaper than those fancy smartphones. And more useful. And if you're reading this right here, if you've somehow magically found out about me, you've basically already passed the most important test. You know how to find good stuff online ;-)...

That's really all you need. And the willingness to learn new things. New skills. And that's already about it. And again, as you're reading this you've basically already passed step one. The second step is to get going.

You can even start if you don't have any skills right now. When I started three years ago all I could do was to write emails and call people. That's all the tangible skills I had when I left business school. I couldn't do anything else, except telling people what to do. That's really all you learn when you major in business.

And 100% of the things I'm doing now are things I haven't learned in school or at university. As a matter of fact, if I had listened to my teachers I would probably never have started writing. I was the worst student in class when it came to writing essays. THE WORST. I almost failed high school because of it. That's how bad I was.

And now most of the things I'm doing are based on things I was pretty bad at when I started. And we're all bad at everything when we're starting. No matter what. We all suck. And the only way to get better at anything is to keep doing it.

I've now been writing for more than three years. But just creating stuff isn't enough. Just like I said earlier. Write it and they will come doesn't work. Just like create it and they will come doesn't work. Or produce it and they will come doesn't work.

That's what I had to learn the hard way when I released my first book in 2013. If you don't have an audience, if you don't know how to send traffic to a website, if you don't know how to setup a simple website, if you don't know how to sell stuff, if you've never sold anything to anyone in your life before then you're pretty much screwed.

I had no clue about any of this back in 2013. So I had to learn all of this. And no one taught me how to do this. I had to learn everything from scratch. And because I was so clueless and didn't have enough money to spend hundreds or maybe even thousands of dollars on online courses, I figured everything out by trial and error.

I went from one thing to the next. I was so insecure about how to price my stuff that in the beginning I gave it away for free. And then I asked people to pay as much as they wanted to. And then I went to $10 ebooks. And then to packages of up to $100.

But it was a very slow process. I basically didn't spend anything on anything. I was bootstrapping everything. And did everything myself. Just until recently I did every little thing myself. Even the covers for my books. I learned how to do all of it. The first time I hired someone to do something for me was to create the cover for this book right here.

If you really want something, you don't need a lot of money. If you really want something bad enough, you'll figure it out. No matter what. And most of the time it's a lot better to be up against the wall. When you don't have a lot of money. When the only option you have is to succeed. Because then you'd have to be creative.

Heck, I got so creative that I'm now even teaching these techniques to other people. Just the other day I got an email from someone who works at a big stock exchange in Europe and she asked me if I could show the companies they've invested in how they can achieve the biggest impact with basically zero cash.

Here's the thing...

The more money you have, the bigger your mistakes will be. But the mistake and the learning will always be the exact same. No matter if you're losing $5 or

$50,000. Sure, you've gotta be wiling to learn from your mistakes first. No matter how big or small. If you don't, then no money in the world will help you.

So why do I think that anyone can do what I've done, no matter where they're from or how much or how little money they have?

Simply because this whole thing is about time. And patience. And consistently putting in the work. And the willingness to learn new things. And getting back up again. Over and over again. There really are no shortcuts. You can't cut corners.

Here's how it really works...

The longer you're around, the more people will know about you. It' simple math. The longer you're around, the more often you're showing up, the more people will take you serious. The more people will start to notice. It's that simple.

Also, you've gotta implement all the things you've learned along the way. And constantly tweak what you're doing. If no one ends up reading your stuff or buying your stuff you know that something might be wrong about it.

And only you can find out what those reasons are. No one else can.

And having a family or a mortgage is no excuse. As a matter of fact that should push you even more. Because your job is not safe. Nothing is safe anymore. And the ONLY way to make sure that you'll always be there for your family is to diversify your income streams. To diversify your risk. Your skills. Your life.

I know it's tough. But that's really the only way.

Who am I to be talking about kids, family and mortgage anyway? I don't have any of this. So what the hell do I know? I don't know anything about it. But I know that if something is important to me, then I won't just one plan.

I'll have many different plans. Especially when my plan A is a very shaky plan based on other people who can fire me whenever they want to. I'll diversify my risk. So when the shit hits the fan I can still be there for that someone. Or those someones...

So when your main source of income disappears, for example your job, you should always have a few more aces up your sleeve. Sure, this is not going to happen over night. This is a year long process. And there's no blueprint for it. It's all about trial & error. And consistency. And never giving up.

And the best thing you can do right now is to keep your job for as long as you can and figure out all of this other stuff on the side. Simply because it's a lot easier to go through a trial & error process when you don't have a gun pointed at your head.

Because when you're trying to figure all of this out, when you don't have a job anymore, when the shit hit the fan, it's like having a gun pointed at your head. And when all you got are a maximum of six attempts until that one bullet in that gun will hit your head, then this is a hell lot of pressure.

Look. It doesn't matter if you're living in the US, India, Germany, China or the Ukraine. You can do this from everywhere. All you need is an internet connection.

You can learn all of these things by either using my approach, which is probably the slower approach and learn everything yourself by trial & error or you take a look at some of the hundreds of online courses out there and then get going and see whether or not those techniques work for you.

Heck. You'd probably be even a lot faster than me. I wasn't able to do anything. I could only tell people how to do things. I could only delegate. And manage. But it's hard to tell people to do things if you don't have money in exchange for the stuff they should do for you.

Many people are already able to do things. Like program stuff. Or design things. This is a hell of a competitive advantage. I didn't know how to do anything. I had to learn everything from scratch.

And again. There are no shortcuts. It will take a while. Probably a lot longer than you might think right now. If you think it'll take 1 year, it'll probably take 10 years. If you think it'll take 2 years, then it might take 5 years. And so on.

And at the end of the day it all boils down to sacrifice. The more you're willing to sacrifice right now, the more work you're willing to put in right now, the more you'll potentially be able to get back further down the road. But there's no guarantee for it. Ever.

I guess it's true what they say...

You've gotta live like no one else ever will for a couple of years, to be able to live the rest of your life like no one else ever can.

Look. Here's how I see things...

If you're not willing to sacrifice anything right now, if you're not willing to sacrifice the dinners with your friends, if you're not willing to sell your car, if you're not willing to move into a smaller apartment, if you're not willing to work 12-16 hours a day for a few years, then you might not be serious enough about it.

Then you might not believe enough in yourself. And if you don't believe in yourself, then no one else ever will.

Over the years so many people have sent me their stuff and asked me for feedback. And I told all of them the same thing. Send me another email when you've written 30 blog posts. Or when you have your first 30 paying clients. Or when you've written your third book.

And guess from how many people I've heard back over the years?

Zero. Yapp. That's right. No one ever got back in touch with me.

And I'll say it again.

Everybody can do what I'm doing. Everybody can do this. Everybody can create his or her own freedom.

But I guarantee you that almost no one ever will...

How to get noticed

No one will magically find out about you. Ever...

And no one magically found out about me either.

This is something I haven't talked about that much, yet. But a lot of people have asked me this in the past. It's the one missing link. It's the missing like of the puzzle. This is what many people have asked me in the past.

And it's one of the only really actionable pieces of advice I give in this book. Because it's the only thing no one out there ever talks about. And I feel that someone should talk about it...

How do you even get noticed? How do you make your ideas spread?

I don't know how to get noticed. I don't know how people might find out about you. I only know what I did. And that's what I'm going to share with you right here.

Look. I get it. Sometimes (well, actually in 99% of the cases) you can put in so much work for so many years and still nothing really happens. And maybe you've even taken a look at all of these online courses out there that want to teach you how to build an audience. How to send traffic to your website or your blog.

But you just can't seem to make it work. And I know. This happens. With almost all of the advice out there on how to build your audience. Or how to send traffic to your site. Most of the advice just doesn't work. Most of the advice comes from people who've never even done it themselves before.

There's so much B.S. out there that won't get you anywhere. That's why I'll share one of my biggest secrets with you on how I started. On how most people found out about me. Maybe that's also how you've found out about me. I don't know.

And it's the same trick over and over again. I've used it on every platform. On Twitter. On Medium. On Quora. Pretty much everywhere I'm active. Even Facebook for a while.

What I do is pretty simple. And no rocket science.

I follow people. Tons of people. Over and over again. And I don't do it for a day or two or so. No. When I decide to focus on a new platform I do it every single day. For at least 2-3 months. Every single day. No matter what.

Here's the thing about the world we live in today...

No one will magically find out about you. No matter how good you are. No matter if you're the best writer out there. No matter if you're the best singer out there. No matter if you have the best product or service out there.

You've gotta do something for it. Sure, you could invest in advertisement if you have a whole lot of money to waste. Which I don't. And you probably also don't have money to waste. Or you could become the protege of someone who pushes your work. Like Tim Ferriss or something. But I have no clue about how that works. But I'm sure it works.

Look. Here's how I see things. When you're an artist, like a singer for example you had to send your demo tapes to record labels. No matter if you were one of the best out there. You had to send them out. Sometimes to hundreds of record labels until someone might call you back.

The same holds true for writers. When you were an author you had to send your book proposals to hundreds and hundreds of publishers. And most of the time you wouldn't even get a response from them.

Or when you had a physical product. You had to to get in touch with hundreds and hundreds of store owners to get it on the shelves. Or hundreds of meetings with some biz dev reps. Either way.

You had to send your stuff out there. No one would ever magically find out about your new product. Your new book. Your new songs. And so on. You had to pass through gatekeepers. Middlemen were controlling the game. And making the rules.

And today, things are different. Today there are no gatekeepers anymore. Today everything is decentralized. Today, there are no middlemen left anymore. Or they have a lot less influence. So instead of getting in touch with the gatekeepers, instead of sending them your work you'd have to send your work to your potential customers, readers or listeners directly.

And because everybody realized that there are basically no gatekeepers anymore, everybody started addressing their potential customers, readers and listeners directly. Actually, there are still gatekeepers. But these are now sort of "democratized" platforms.

But because everybody realized this huge opportunity, the opportunity that you can now directly reach millions of people without a gatekeeper through platforms like YouTube, Twitter, Facebook and also Medium, it gets harder and harder every single day to get noticed.

Because everybody is now fighting for your reader's, customer's or listeners attention. Simply designing a t-shirt and putting it on a platform like Teespring won't do anything. Just like publishing a great article on Medium won't do anything. Or putting a video on YouTube. Or publishing a book on Amazon.

Simply because there are millions and millions of t-shirts, articles, books, products, videos or what not out there. And tens of thousands are released every single day. So no one will even notice that you exist. No one. No matter how good you are. You need leverage first.

That's why it's so important that you send your stuff to people. And the way to do it today, the way how I do it is to follow people. Tons of people. Because then a lot of people will check out your profile. Check out your stuff. Maybe click on a link or two. And some of them will follow you back.

And then it's about putting out great stuff over and over again. I put out stuff every single day. Sure, not all of it is great. But I try. It's all just a numbers game. I think I said this in an earlier article already.

People's timelines and newsfeeds are so crowded that it's very likely that they're not going to see your first update. It's also very likely that they're not going to see your second, third, fourth or maybe even fifth update of the week. But it's really hard to miss all of your 7 updates of the week.

But they need to see your stuff as much as possible. Because it builds up trust. And anticipation. It creates real fans. If they don't see your stuff, they'll never become true fans. That's why publishing one update a week won't be enough anymore. Especially on these crowded platforms. That's why doing what everybody else is doing isn't enough anymore. No matter what it is you're doing.

And I get it. Many successful people will tell you that all you'd have to do is to create super great content. To be authentic. To create great products. To create great customer experience. To have the best what not. And so on. And you know what? Everybody reads the same advice. And everybody applies the same advice. So at the end of the day it wont help you to stand out anymore.

But here's the biggest problem they don't tell you...

You'll be competing with them (the gurus) on every new platform out there. And by the way, they blast out at least 3-4 updates A DAY on most of the platforms. And here's why you'll directly be competing with all the people or companies out there who are already successful, who already have an audience.

Because they can easily leverage their existing audience on that new, new platform. They can easily send out an email to their followers that they're now on Medium, or on Snapchat. Or what not.

That's a leverage you'll never ever have when you're starting from scratch. Whatever it is that you're trying to start from scratch. You'll always be competing with the big brands. The mega influencers. The best selling authors.

And not only this. The leverage they already have will lead to even more leverage because their existing fans will like their stuff, spread their stuff, hit that share button and then they'll reach even more people.

That's not unfair or anything. That's just the way it works. You've gotta build your audience once and once you were able to successfully do so you can leverage that audience over and over again. You've gotta put in the work. If you're not willing to put in the work, then don't complain about things being rigged or unfair.

Everybody who's now on top came from the exact same spot you're at right now. The exact same spot I still am right now. They came from the bottom. And worked their way to the top.

And most of the time, the best way to build your first audience is by being the first on a new platform. The first who offers incredible value. The first to offer really good stuff. And once you've done that, you can leverage it over and over again.

That's what Gary Vee has done on Twitter as he says. That's what James Altucher has done with his blog and the huge email list he now has. They built their audience on one platform and now they can then simply leverage that platform. Over and over again.

By the way, if you're reading this on Medium, Medium has even a built in leverage. Medium let's you sign up with your Twitter account and then it will automatically follow everyone who follows you on Twitter. Or they will automatically follow you. Either way.

That's a huge leverage. Because it allows you to automatically transport your audience from Twitter onto Medium. That's what gave me a leverage, also. When I signed up with my Twitter account I automatically had a few thousand followers without ever having written a single piece of content.

So how did I get so many Twitter followers? By following thousands of people every single day. And then some of them followed back. And then I signed up to Medium with that Twitter account and BOOM, I had a few thousand followers.

And then I followed more people on Medium. Over and over again. And then I started writing one article a day. And that's what I've done ever since. That's what I've done on basically every platform out there.

Will it still work when you read this?

Maybe. Maybe not. But if you're really good it will still work. On every platform. Until organic reach will be capped. Just like it was capped on Facebook fan pages a few years ago.

That's why It's so important that once you were able to build up momentum on one platform that you already start using your leverage for the next platform that will come.

And it will come. For sure.

And that's how you get noticed.

That's how you get noticed when you don't have a lot of cash and create good shit.

No matter if you're a brand or a person...

The ultimate cheat sheet to absolute freedom

There's no such thing as freedom...

it starts in your head

Freedom is not given to you. Ever. No matter which country you live in. Or where you're from. Freedom is something you've gotta take. No one is going to give you anything. Freedom is a conscious decision.

plant seeds

You've gotta start planting seeds. Seeds that might maybe one day turn into a strong enough tree. No matter how big or small. Every opportunity you create for yourself and the people around you, every thought or idea you share with the world, every conversation you have is a seed planted. A seed planted in your head. In other people's heads. Everywhere.

perfection

Perfection will only hold you back. From what? From everything...

no reason

You don't have to have a reason for everything. Or justify why you did something. Or did not do something. Sometimes things happen for no reason at all. Like not wanting to talk to someone. Or not willing to meet up with someone. For no reason at all. And that's totally fine. That's real freedom.

trading time

Trading time for money is not freedom. As a matter of fact it's a prison. Because the only way you'll ever be able to make more money is to trade more of your time. And then you'll have even less time. Which means that you'll be less free than ever before. But you need money. To be able to buy yourself some freedom. And that's the riddle. That's the maze. You've gotta find ways to stop trading your time for money or else you'll never be free. You've gotta be willing to work a few years on that. Because that's how long it'll take you to figure out how it really works.

ignore everybody

Ignore everybody who's trying to give you advice on what you should do but has never done what you're doing or want to do. Ignore your parents, your friends and pretty much everybody else out there. Only listen to the people who've either successfully or unsuccessfully done what you're doing or are about to do.

have enough

Sometimes freedom is about having enough. What does that even mean? It means that at one point you've gotta have enough. Enough of what? Of everything...

reinvention

Freedom is about reinvention. Over and over again. It's not about doing the same things over and over again. You've gotta keep reinventing yourself. Even, no especially when a reinvention fails. You've gotta be willing to go from employee to entrepreneur. From entrepreneur to standup comedian. And from there to running a restaurant. And then to... But what do I know? Just shake things up every once in a while or your freedom might turn into a prison.

other people's freedom

Help other people to create their freedom. So you can see and learn how it's done.

entrepreneurship

Being an entrepreneur is not equal to freedom. As a matter of fact, being an entrepreneur is a prison in disguise. Instead of depending on your company, you'd be depending on your clients. Or investors. Or other people who give you their hard earned dollars. And because they pay you their own money and not some imaginary company dollars, it'll be a lot harder to satisfy them. To even get them to pay you something in the first place...

don't be someone else

If you're trying to be someone you're not, if you're doing something just because you like the result, then you won't make it. Simply because if you do something just for the result of it, then you'll be doing something that you don't really enjoy doing. You might start the next Kickstarter for food. Just because you like where Kickstarter is now. But if you don't absolutely love food, if you're not 100% food, then you'd never be able to make it through the tough times. Chasing opportunities never works. Only doing stuff you genuinely enjoy doing works. In the long run...

if it's easy

If it's easy it will probably not work anymore and not lead to freedom. Simply because if something is easy, the window of opportunity closes the millisecond it opens.

not knowing

Not knowing is freedom. Realizing that you don't know a thing about anything might be the most liberating thing in the world. That's real freedom. Now get out there and start doing and learn more so you know more...

people matter

It matters who you hang out with. If you hang out with negative people you'll become negative yourself. If you work with small minded people, you'll become small minded yourself. It all rubs off. And if you live in a country where there aren't (or you think there aren't) that many great people you'd like to hang out with, or they simply don't want to hang out with you, then follow all of their stuff online. Create your virtual team.

money

Most people get money wrong. Money is not for buying things. Because things don't make us happy. Maybe they do. But just for two seconds. Money is for buying ourselves some freedom to do the things that make us happy. That's real freedom.

bad days

Freedom is when you allow yourself to have a bad day. Days where you just sit in front of your laptop and binge watch Netflix. Where you do nothing. And that's ok. We all have bad days. Just today, I didn't do anything. Except reading a bit, writing this and hitting the refresh button every once in a while to see if I was able to sell a few more things. And that's ok. As long as you don't regret it. Because that regret will destroy all the fun today and take away all of your energy from tomorrow. So have a few bad days every once in a while. With no regrets...

no time

If you say you have no time for all of this, then you'll never be free.

talent

Talent doesn't matter. Just like intelligence doesn't matter. We all suck when we start something new. It's all about persistence. Consistency. Showing up over and over again. Learning from our mistakes and failures. And getting back up again. Over and over again...

10+ years

It doesn't happen over night. Nothing happens over night. It all takes time. How much time? More than you ever thought possible. Because not only do you have to learn new things, not only do you have to apply these new things, but you'd have to reprogram your brain. You'd have to unlearn all the crap that was put into your brain for the past 10, 20, 30 or maybe even more years.

#sacrifice

It's all just a matter of how much you're willing to give up right now. How much you're willing to sacrifice over the next few years. It's about living a life for a few years like no one else ever will, so you might maybe have a shot at living a life no one else ever can. And I'm not talking about living in a box for a few years. I'm talking about putting in the work. But what if I want to party with my friends? Come back and read this again in one year. Or two years. Or three years. Or maybe never read this ever again...

your three things

Are the most important thing...

But then again. I don't know. There's no blueprint. There's no guidebook to follow. There's just figuring out what works for you and what doesn't. Everything right here worked for me. Maybe it will also work for you. Maybe not.

But most importantly, you've gotta get out there and start writing your own cheat sheet. You've gotta start writing your own book. You've gotta start shooting your own movie. You've gotta start investing in yourself and buy yourself some freedom.

Or just keep doing what you're already doing. Maybe you already have everything you need and just haven't realized it, yet...

Outro

This is the original post I wrote one month before I started writing this book. This is how everything started. This is what inspired me to write this short book. This is it...

I've basically lived out of a backpack for the past 7 years.

It all started in 2009. I moved to Shanghai as an exchange student. I planned to stay there for a few months . And those few months turned into almost two years.

I started a clothing company. Which my partner and I had to shutdown because it didn't work out. I also taught English on the side because I needed to make some extra cash.

Because cash is king. Always.

And when you're starting a company and want to be able to pay for food at the same time, the only thing you really need is cash. Everything else doesn't really matter.

It doesn't really matter where that cash comes from. It doesn't matter where the paycheck comes from. Be it that burger joint. That fancy bank or that dodgy language school. As long as it's legal. And it pays enough to get by.

During those two years I basically lived out of a backpack with less than 10kg of stuff. That's all I really needed. And it was still too much stuff.

I lived at four or five different places during those two years. I don't even remember all the places anymore. I lived there with other people so I never paid more than 250 bucks rent a month. All places were furnished. I never bought furniture in my life.

One place was taken over by a pimp and his hookers while I was in Germany trying to figure out how I could get my degree. In the end I got my degree. But I didn't get my shoes back. Or my electric shaver. And a few other things.

So for the next few months I was always looking at people's shoes to maybe find that one guy who took my shoes. I never found that guy. Or my shoes…

In 2011 I had to move back to Germany because I was using more money every month than I was making. A clear sign that something is wrong. That your business might just not be working out. Ever.

So I started working for a big corporation. I lived in many different places for the next 18 months or so. Cologne, Munich, Berlin and New York. Again, I was basically living out of a backpack. In furnished apartments. And saved basically almost everything I made.

Luckily that apartment in New York was paid for by that company. I would never have been able to pay for it. I liked living there. A lot. Especially with all the restaurants in Hell's Kitchen, the area where I lived.

They had 3 Thai restaurants right next to the place I lived. I think they had 3 different ones. But I'm not 100% sure. They were all called Bangkok. I think they were called Bangkok I, Bangkok II and Bangkok III. I got take home food from either I, II or III almost every night after work.

And you know what?

I'm writing this piece right here while sitting in a coffee shop in Bangkok. The real Bangkok. Not I, II or III. The real deal.

And I guess it's true what they say. If you can make it here (New York) you can make it anywhere. I didn't make it there. I quit my job and moved back to Germany.

I moved back in with my girlfriend of that time where I lived for a few months. Until we broke up. I think I'm a terrible roommate. And I have the tendency to just move in with people without them even realizing it. Until it's too late. For them. For me. For everyone.

A friend of mine has a sticker that says "I like to be alone but I don't want to be lonely." I think that's very true for most of us…

So some time between moving back to Germany and moving in with my girlfriend of that time I quit my job and started working on my first book. I didn't know anything about writing back then.

And I still don't know a thing about writing three years later.

I didn't even know what exactly I'd be writing about in that book. I thought it would take me three months to write it. In the end it took me more than ten months to write it and it cost me more than just a relationship.

On the flip side I made around $5000 with that book. Not a whole lot. But still a lot more than what an average author makes with an ebook. A lousy $300.

So I had to move back in with my mom where I stayed for a while. And I still stay there whenever I'm in Germany. Simply because I don't own any furniture. Also, I don't feel like paying 4 months of rent just to be able to move into a new place. Without any furniture…

And once that first book was done I decided to travel a bit. After all I didn't have anything or anyone holding me back in Germany. I didn't have a job, no girlfriend and my friends were basically busy working all the time.

So I traveled across Europe and gave talks in all sorts of countries that I've never been to before. Why? Well, simply because I wanted to see how it was like.

I went to the Czech Republic. To Poland. To Hungary. To Slovenia. To Romania. To Serbia. To Bosnia. And a few other places in the region.

I spent less than $600 a month and covered close to 9000km by bus and train. Some folks paid me to give talks. Some didn't. But that didn't really matter that much.

What mattered was that I did something just because I felt like doing it. For no particular reason at all. Just because I could. And I think that's the secret.

To what?

To all of it I guess…

We all can, if we really want to.

So once that tour was over I continued doing whatever I felt like doing. Just because I could.

And ever since I'm everywhere and nowhere. And I own nothing and everything...

More about Yann

Oh hey. Yann here... I guess I should introduce myself, so here we go...

I tell the truth, write essays on how to kick ass in life, business and as an entrepreneur. I also build online businesses & help others build theirs. Over the past few years I've worked with hundreds of entrepreneurs, was a keynote speaker at top tier conferences, built an audience of more than 140.000 monthly readers across multiple platforms, wrote seven books and mentor(ed) at dozens of startup accelerators and incubators worldwide. And most importantly...

I'm everywhere and nowhere. And I own nothing and everything...

Also, feel free to reach out to say hi and send me an email to yann@girard.net or visit my website at www.yanngirard.com

I'm everywhere and nowhere. And I own nothing and everything.

Printed in Great Britain
by Amazon